ESSENTIAL LEGAL SKILLS

Problem Solving

Margot Costanzo

with Tim Lindsey

Series Editor
JULIE MACFARLANE

Cavendish
Publishing
Limited

First published in Great Britain 1995 by Cavendish Publishing Limited,
The Glass House, Wharton Street, London WC1X 9PX
Telephone: 071-278 8000 Facsimile: 071-278 8080

British Library Cataloguing in Publication Data

Costanzo, M
Problem Solving - (Essential Legal Skills Series)
I Title II Series
340.11

ISBN 1-874241-46-5

Cover photograph by Jerome Yeats
Printed and bound in Great Britain

Contents

Preface

This book started as a feeling of irritation and disappointment in law school. These feelings have given way to fascination and interest. There is fascination for the gap between what lawyers say they do and what they actually do. There is interest in the challenge to explain the intuitive and what is often accepted by talented lawyers as just common sense.

This and the book on legal writing were written in just over two years with the help and support of many people. First, with the unknowing participation of all the fine law graduates who have attended courses that I have run over the last 15 years. Second, with the active support of Professor Neil Gold and the City Polytechnic of Hong Kong who gave me the opportunity to consult on the topic of creativity in problem solving during the design process for the Postgraduate Certificate of Laws. Third, with risk taking by Steven Warshal from Centaur Conferences who gave me the opportunity to give the paper that was the germ for this book in 1991. Fourthly, with the active support of many people. From the United Kingdom I thank the Legal Education and Training Group, especially Professor Sherr, Dr Alexandrina le Clezio, Sally Woodward, Jenny Chapman, Helena Twist and Roger Trussell; also Professor William Twining and Hilary Lewis Ruttley; and, last but not least, Roger G Butterworth from Simmons & Simmons who provided the model letter featured in the Legal Writing book which is truly a model. From Canada I thank Ruth Windeler, Professor Mary Gold and Paul M Perell. From Australia I thank Dr Alan Tapper, Ronwyn North, Dick McCann, Rob Perry and Mrs Ada Moshinsky QC.

Minter Ellison and Morris Fletcher deserve a special thanks; to Rob Stewart for the support in all courses developed over the years that fed into this book; to Fay O'Grady, Ro Hay, Prue Presser, Lyn Newlands and Shaunnagh Harte who organised all those inter-library loans and forgave all those overdue books; to

Phillip Greenham, David Curtis, David Grant, Tom Bradley, Margaret Calvert and Linda Berry who provided material for the problem solving book; to Michael Whalley and Stephen Britt who provided me with an office when in London, allowed much of the manuscript to go back and forth in firm courier bags, and counselled me about photos of Fleet Street.

An author who can think and talk but not draw must be grateful to an illustrator who can do all of these things. Shortly before the completion of this book, Tim Lindsey completed his PhD in Indonesian Studies while running an active practice as a barrister at the Victorian Bar, collaborating on a number of other book projects and occasionally helping out in the graphic design business he helped to establish as a student. I hope the fun we had in discussing the graphics is communicated in some of the pictures. Stephen O'Connor at Artifishal Studios typeset the model and dithering devices with great speed and forbearance. James Stephenson drew the model in Chapter 9 and prepared the animation art work. He even managed to hold up a fair pretence that he found some interest in the project!

An author in Australia with a publisher in the United Kingdom and an editor in Canada who was in Hong Kong for a time must give thanks to fax, phone and international courier. Dr Julie Macfarlane and I had many agreeable disagreements; her incisive comments cut through my own dithering so that the works worked on. Jo Reddy and Sonny Leong at Cavendish and their staff were ever courteous, supportive and patient through the postponed deadlines.

It is traditional to say that these people contributed much to any virtues that the works may possess but are not responsible for their many faults. In this case, it is also true.

A final tribute to my children Luca and Vanessa who bore my absences with bemused tolerance. And to Maria Costanzo, their grandmother, who shouldered many of the tasks reserved for a parent with dignity, grace and love.

Melbourne
December 1994

Editor's Introduction

'The essence of our lawyer's craft lies in skills ...; in practical, effective, persuasive, inventive skills for getting things done ...'

Karl Llewellyn

The appearance of this new series of texts on legal skills reflects the recent shift in emphasis in legal education away from a focus on teaching legal information and towards the teaching and learning of task-related and problem-solving skills.

Legal education in the United Kingdom has undergone significant changes over the past ten years as a result of growing concern, expressed for the most part by the profession, over its adequacy to prepare students for the practice of law. At the same time, many legal educators have voiced fears that concentrating on drilling students in substantive law promotes neither the agility of mind nor the development of judgment skills which provide the basis for continued learning.

Today courses providing clinical experience and instruction in legal skills are increasingly a part of undergraduate law programmes. Both branches of the profession in England and Wales have fundamentally revised the content and format of their qualifying courses to include direct instruction in practical skills. In Scotland, the Diploma in Legal Practice, which emphasises the learning of practical skills, has been in place since 1980/81.

Nonetheless, legal skills education in the United Kingdom is still in its infancy. Much is to be learned from other jurisdictions which have a longer history of the use of practical and experience-based teaching methods, lessons invaluable to UK law teachers many of whom now face the challenge of developing new courses on legal skills. The ready exchange of ideas between skills teachers in the United Kingdom and abroad is an important part of the development process. So too is the generation of 'home-grown' texts and materials designed specifically for legal skills education in undergraduate and professional schools in the United Kingdom.

The introduction of skills teaching into the legal education curriculum has implications not only for what students learn in law school but also for how they learn. Similarly it has implications for the kind of textbooks which will be genuinely useful to students who wish to succeed in these programmes.

This new series of texts seeks to meet this need. Each text leads the reader through a stage-by-stage model of the development of a particular legal skill; from planning, through implementation in a variety of guises, to evaluation of performance. Each contains numerous practical exercises and guides to improve practice. Each draws on a network of theories about effective legal practice and relates theory to practice where that is useful and relevant.

The authors are all skills teachers with many years of practical experience at all levels of legal education. They draw on relevant literature and practice from all over the common law world. However each book is written specifically for students of law and legal practice in the United Kingdom and sets learning in the context of English law and against the backdrop of the Law Society's standards for the new Legal Practice Courses, due to commence in 1993/4.

Each of these texts is designed for use either as a supplement to a legal skills course taught at an undergraduate or professional level, or as a model for the structure and content of the course itself. We recommend the use of these books, therefore, to students and skills teachers alike, and hope that you enjoy them.

Julie Macfarlane
London, Ontario
January 1993

CHAPTER

1

From Method to Mêlée

'Law is not a sacred text, however, but a usually humdrum social practice vaguely bound by ethical and political convictions. The soundness of legal interpretations and other legal propositions is best gauged, therefore, by an examination of their consequences in a world of fact.'

Richard A Posner (1990)

1.1 The importance of professional problem solving

In 1927 Carrie Buck was sterilised under a sterilisation law in the State of Virginia. Carrie had scored a mental age of nine under the Stanford-Binet scale. Her mother, then 52, scored a mental age of seven. In upholding the validity of the law, the famous American judge Oliver Wendell Holmes Jr, said:

> We have seen more than once that the public welfare may call upon the best citizens for their lives. It would be strange if it could not call upon those who already sap the strength of the state for these lesser sacrifices ... Three generations of imbeciles are enough.

Buck v Bell **274 US 200 (1927)**

There were 7,500 people in the State of Virginia who were also sterilised under the same rule between 1924 and 1975. The operations were performed primarily on white men and women considered feeble-minded and anti-social, including 'unwed mothers, prostitutes, petty criminals and children with disciplinary problems'. Carrie's sister, Doris, was also sterilised. She was told that the operation was for an appendix and a rupture. Not one of the physicians consulted for infertility during her childbearing years at three hospitals recognised that her fallopian tubes had been severed (Gould (1981) p 335).

Carrie and Doris bore the brunt of the combined efforts of legal and medical problem solving with quiet resignation. With the benefit of hindsight, their story is both tragic and terrible. Professional practice includes learning by trial and error. The trial for the client might last until the end of their days, while the error will just be another learning experience in the busy day of the professional.

Until recently, the market economy seems to have had little impact on professional practice. Medical and legal practice remained a seller's market for much longer than the selling of commodities or computers. In a seller's market, the seller determines what the buyer ought to buy, on what terms the purchase should be made, and what constitutes a valid product or service. Now, even for the professions, it is a buyer's market. Clients have opinions both about the outcomes of our attempts at problem solving, and about the processes we put our clients through. The buyers are designing processes they prefer and the professions are adopting them.

Alternate dispute resolution is one such example. More than 100 years after Dickens pointed out the labyrinthine inefficiencies of the British system of civil procedure, and in spite of many lawyers' attempts to overhaul and simplify resolution of disputes by the courts, clients were moved to design a substitute system. For example, in the early 1980s, as a co-operative exercise by America's largest public companies, The Center for Public Resources, was formed. The Center established an alternative dispute resolution programme for legal disputes and invited lawyers and other professionals to be involved in the design of resolution techniques. A decade later, law firms publicise their skills in alternate dispute resolution as though they were its authors.

Problem solving can be *legal*, not only because it involves lawyers but also because it involves the law. We can no longer assume that all problems that can be solved through the law or legal processes will be solved by lawyers. Business people, psychologists and accountants are also legal problem solvers. It is increasingly likely that the definitions of successful problem solving will need to accommodate both the demands of the client and techniques from other disciplines.

1.2 What is problem solving?

1.2.1 Distinction between a problem to be solved and a situation to be managed

Some definitions of problem solving restrict the expression to situations in which something has already gone wrong (Kepner & Tregoe (1981)). A situation to be managed is different from a problem to be solved. A problem to be solved usually involves a deviation in the past, or anticipating deviations in the future. Under this definition, a client issued with a summons for drink driving would require a lawyer to act as a problem solver. A situation to be managed, on the other hand, usually involves steps to be taken for the future. The same client who wanted advice on how to establish a business to minimise personal liability to trade creditors would have a situation to be managed, not a problem to be solved.

1.2.2 Problem solving versus creative thinking

Another approach is to distinguish situations applying established professional knowledge and methodologies to solve a problem, from situations requiring the thinker to search for new knowledge and new methodologies. The former is called *problem solving* and the latter is called *creative thinking*. It is problematic for professional problem solvers to call their work creative problem solving. Creativity, in part, recognises that a better answer might only be revealed through error. Creativity requires a climate in which the decision maker is encouraged to take risk.

1.2.3   Problem solving in the context of a particular skill

Some approaches include problem solving as one component in a useful skill. Fisher and Ury's book *Getting to Yes* (1982) sets out an approach to any negotiation which they describe as both principled and problem solving. The participants are cast in the role of problem solvers because they aim for:

- a wise outcome reached efficiently and amicably;
- a process which focuses on interests of the parties, not their positions;
- all parties accepting responsibility for inventing acceptable options;
- an outcome that can be validated against objective standards.

The negotiation might involve events in the past which could be described as a deviation, or might involve an agreement to be reached governing future rights, obligations and agreed procedures (see above para 1.2.1).

1.2.4   Two kinds of legal problem solving

Nathanson (1989) sees legal problem solving as *client goals impeded by obstacles*. Legal problems can involve both *playing out conflict decisions* (found in litigation, negotiation and other forms of dispute resolution) and *conflict blocking decisions* (in which the lawyer tries to meet client goals by minimising risk and potential conflict) (p 123).

All commentators agree that problem solving is a complex process. Teachers and other commentators have naturally extracted some elements that they can deal with and concentrated on them. The problem is that the teacher remains in the classroom with the simplification, while the practitioner faces the complexity.

1.3   Problem solving as mess

Donald A Schon observed (1983):

> The situations of practice are not problems to be solved but problematic situations characterised by uncertainty, disorder and indeterminacy.

The young lawyer, originally attracted to the study of law for its promise of order and predictability, is often dismayed to find that the practice of law is anything but ordered and predictable. The concentration of law study on appellate cases means that many law graduates come to private practice unaware that being a lawyer involves a process of blocking conflict as well as processes for playing conflict out (see above para 1.2.4). They are often unaware of the sheer volume of legal work in private practice that involves structuring a client's transactions for the future rather than advocating about client's actions in the past. Uneducated in psychology, sheltered from poverty and despair (above para 1.2.1) by a comfortable bookishness, and without practice in dealing with the painful and violent aspects of life, young graduates are often at a loss to see law as helpful. And their clients don't care what the law says. They want to know what they should do.

Russell Ackoff, quoted in Schon (1983) described the problems facing operations research as *messes*. This description applies to the sort of problem solving facing legal practitioners. He went on to say that:

> Problems are abstractions extracted from messes by analysis ...

Most legal practitioners could relate to the description of the problems they have to solve as messes. Lawyers always say that no two legal problems are the same. Many legal problems need to be solved by a combination of applying existing knowledge and methodologies (*traditional problem solving*) and by seeking knowledge unfamiliar to that lawyer from other disciplines and by designing new methodologies (*creative problem solving* (above para 1.2.2)). Whether professional problem solving is judged successful or otherwise, will partly depend on the problem extracted by the professional from the mess.

Donald Schon characterises education for professionals as the technical rationality of a rule-based system. He describes practice as reflective artistry in which the professional is often required to devise techniques and to solve unfamiliar problems on the spot. By implication, therefore, Schon suggests that professional problem solving is more like creative problem solving that we might at first have thought. The suggestion inevitably is that education in technical rationality does not prepare professionals for successful problem solving through reflective artistry.

From the client perspective, lawyers need to achieve an outcome which is professionally responsible and satisfies the client in terms of suitability, time and cost.

Problem solving can also be evaluated from an internal, professional perspective. Problems need to be solved within the broad client problem. Which information is relevant? How must the lawyer act to be professionally responsible? What is the precise formulation and meaning of particular laws? What are alternative formulations which might be more just? What are possible methods of implementation and their validity? Sometimes these professional debates seem to the client to take precedence over arriving at the solution he or she requires.

Clients judge the success of legal problem solving only from their perspective. Lawyers need to take into account both perspectives. Sometimes the professional dimension is so complex, the client perspective recedes.

Some examples of this multi-dimensional character of legal problem solving might make this point clearer.

When George Coode was asked to prepare a digest of the Poor Laws, he felt it necessary to publish a monograph on techniques of good legislative drafting as a preface to the laws.

First published in 1842, his was the first in a long line of attempts to simplify and clarify legal expression. His problem-within-the-problem was determining a valid means of expressing laws clearly and comprehensively. Other lawyers charged with digesting the law may not have performed this additional task.

When May Donoghue drank that fateful bottle of ginger beer containing the snail, her solicitor had two problems-within-the-problem to solve.

First, how to finance the suit: 'I am very poor,' swore May Donoghue poignantly in her Affidavit to The House of Lords, 'and have not in all the world the sum of five pounds'. In fact during the course of the suit, in which Mrs Donoghue won at first instance and then lost 2-1 on appeal, cost orders of nearly £100 sterling were ordered against Mrs Donoghue where she was only claiming a total of £500 sterling. The second internal problem was how to overcome the precedent set by a previous very similar case also taken by Mr Leechman on behalf of a client, in which the client lost.

George Coode took up the questions of *formulating the law* and the *methods* a lawyer should use in so doing. Mr Leechman challenged whether the existing state of the law was fair and offered in argument *an alternative vision* of what the law should be.

These examples give rise to efforts we would characterise as legal problem solving. In each case, the problems to be solved had to be extracted from life by the practitioners. Different practitioners might have extracted different problems from the same mess. Perhaps another drafter would have re-written the Poor Laws without the monograph. Perhaps any other Scottish lawyer would have advised May Donoghue that she had no case. What we extract from the mess as a problem to be solved depends on how we see our role, what we perceive as relevant facts, how we conceive appropriate solutions and how much we involve the client in the process.

1.4   Legal problem solving in a mêlée

Conventional approaches to teaching legal problem solving hark back to the era of technical rationality in science developed in the 19th century. Science offered techniques for rational analysis of phenomena. Analysis of case law and statute became the lawyer's microscope. The application of rules, principles and policies, thus extracted, to given fact situations either under the torch of Socratic dialogue, or in the examination room, became the lawyer's controlled laboratory experiment.

Science has moved on. Chaos theory allows scientists to study complex phenomena in the mess of life, rather than requiring the abstraction of a simpler problem from the mess. Chaos theory is being applied to the weather, the turbulence of fluids, the rise and fall of animal populations. Small changes in these systems provoke consequences far in excess of those which might have been predicted by probability theory. Scientists call these *chaotic systems* and are developing new, more complex techniques for studying them and for predicting their behaviour. Chaos theory finds an explanation in their behaviour at the microscopic level that so far has resisted explanation at the macroscopic level (Gleick (1988)).

Jurisprudence has also moved on. Sampford (1989) argues that none of the existing jurisprudential theories alone account for all the elements in the phenomenon of law as we know it. Each theory, therefore, emphasises, and perhaps validates, only some of the problem solving skills actually used in practice.

Sampford describes contemporary legal theory as falling into three categories:

- Positivist theories of legal system, based on rules or norms and concerned to identify the source of authority from which norms or rules derive their applicability. (When a lawyer solves a relatively simple legal problem by applying facts to a statute or regulation, using Aristotelian deductive reasoning to reach a conclusion, legal problem solving resembles the positivist pyramid.)

- Content theories of legal system, containing rules or norms, but based on more general principles and judicial decisions concerned to identify how all elements in the system achieve cohesion and can be justified. (When a lawyer reconciles seemingly inconsistent cases by reformulating a common ratio as an overarching principle at a higher level of generality using Baconian induction, legal problem solving often resembles features of the content theories.)

- Sociological theories of legal system, based on the roles and behaviour of the people in the system and concerned to identify how different people can behave in different ways when confronted with the same legal problem. (When a lawyer has to predict the behaviour of a bureaucrat or judge, or is involved in designing procedures to be followed by an institution or group of institutions, legal problem-solving resembles features of the sociological theories.)

Sampford sketches a non-systematic theory of law, which sees law as one of the manifestations of social relations between individuals involved with the law, 'in all their variety and complexity and especially asymmetric tendencies'. He sees some relations involving rules that provide reasons for action even though the rules will not be shared by all the actors. Law is both disordered by the conflicting relationships with other institutions, and disordering in its own effects. He summarises law as follows:

> The overall image is of a vast web of relations (or, perhaps a multi-dimensional maze) which link directly and indirectly vast numbers of legal officials to each other and to the citizens they affect and by whom they are affected.

Professor Sampford's description offers some insight into the nature of law as a legal mêlée and legal problem solving:

- as *a description* of the complexity of law from the perspective of the social observer;

- as *a listing of methods* used in legal problem solving;

- as *an explanation* of the motives of people obeying, transgressing and applying the law, describing both multiplicity and contradiction which occur in real life.

Issues which are relevant to an understanding of problem solving in the legal mêlée include:

- the role of the law as reason for action;
- the role of argument based on law as persuasion to action;
- the motives of legal decision makers in selecting, accepting or rejecting action;
- the different roles and cultures of the institutions in which legal problem solvers make decisions.

Legal problem solving, in all its dimensions, requires techniques to deal with information, people and the problem solver. Successful legal problem solving should take into account:

- techniques lawyers use consciously;
- techniques lawyers use, but do not talk about;
- techniques from other disciplines;
- ways of avoiding mistakes in problem solving.

This bundle of techniques includes all the skills of how to find and to apply legal rules or principles. It also includes techniques which can enable the lawyer to see himself or herself as part of the problem. Perception, memory and common mistakes in processing information will all be important. Preferred thinking styles and personality preferences of the problem solver might influence which problem is extracted from the mess and which solution is recommended. Problem solving in the legal mêlée will also invite the client's perspective, since the legal mêlée sees the law as only one path of many.

1.5   The rest of this book

The rest of this book surveys techniques which might be of assistance to young legal practitioners either in private practice, or in public service, when they come to solve problems at their desks. I have taken information and techniques from a wide range of disciplines, selected on the basis of their usefulness in practice. Often they are techniques that lawyers employ but do not talk about.

- Chapters 2 and 3 place the lawyer inside the problem.

- Chapter 2 looks at distortions in vision, perception and intuitive judgment that might affect the lawyer, the client or the witness.

- Chapter 3 surveys some theories about preferences in thinking and personality that affect the selection of the problem extracted from the mess.

Chapter 4 looks at legal reasoning from the perspective of the individual lawyer problem solver, with a blank page and a problem. It considers a number of models for general and legal problem solving. The models *list methods* and *range their use over time*, presenting problem solving as a phased and repeatable process.

Chapters 5 to 8 discuss problem solving by reference to one such model. Each chapter examines one step in a four step process. Each chapter deals with the content that the legal problem solver needs to keep in mind, the general thinking processes, and provides some special thinking tools that are particularly appropriate for that step.

Chapter 9 revisits the question of a model for the lawyer problem solver. It proposes the basis of a model that is more complete, dynamic, complex but user friendly.

1.6   End of chapter references and additional reading

Burns, Peter (ed) (1991)   *Donoghue v Stevenson and The Modern Law of Negligence*

Fisher and Ury (1982)   *Getting to Yes* Hutchinson Business

Gleick, James
(1988)
Chaos
Cardinal Sphere Books London

Gould, Stephen Jay
(1981)
The Mismeasure of Man
Penguin Books

Kepner, Charles H
Tregoe, Benjamin B
(1981)
The New Rational Manager
Princeton Press, US

Nathanson, Stephen
(1989)
Problem Solving in Professional Legal Education
Journal of Professional Legal Education
p 121

Posner, Richard A
(1990)
The Problems of Jurisprudence
Harvard University Press

Robinson, Stanley
(1973)
Drafting
Butterworths (Appendix A)

Sampford, Charles
(1989)
The Disorder of Law
Basil Blackwell Ltd, Oxford

Schon, David A
(1983)
The Reflective Practitioner
Basic Books

The Continuing Legal
Society of British
Columbia
(1991)
The Proceedings of the Paisley Conference on the Law of Negligence

CHAPTER

2   The Lawyer Inside the Problem I

'To see red
To see blood
To see light
To see light at the end of the tunnel
To see the score
To see the writing on the wall.'

From *Metaphors: An Annotated Dictionary*

2.1   Perception, conception and intuition

If law is an activity and not just a set of concepts, as Posner suggests, then how the legal mind in the sensory body captures information and processes it will be as potentially relevant to any decision, as the rules and concepts written in the law books.

The lawyer conceives a client problem by sensory *perception* and cerebral *conception*. We tend to focus more on the brain work than on the work of the senses but habitually adapt language from the senses of sight, sound, smell, touch and taste to express this brain work. When we say that we *see blood*, we may not be talking surgery, any more than *seeing the score* implies Mahler. How the lawyer sees the problem will depend on the information the lawyer takes in through the senses and what the lawyer already knows or deems important in the mind. The lawyer, therefore, will be just as subject to distortions in perception as will the client or the witness, but will often be less aware of his or her own distortions than those of others.

Some distortions are attributable to the acquisition of information through the senses; some to the processing of information so acquired. Research into the processes of input and recall of sensory information, and into the processing of ambiguous problems, reports two things in common. First, the cohesive and complete narrative will be convincing either in witness recall or in argument. Second, when the particular perception or instance of intuitive problem solving is compared to what seem to be the facts, there is a departure from objectivity more often than we would like to think.

This chapter contains a summary of some research into perception and intuitive problem solving, with some demonstrations allowing you to test the theories. It sets out some tips for lawyers which you can bear in mind in practice. Use this information like the rules of grammar and syntax in the revision of your thinking and as a viewing point from which to check your progress during the process of problem solving.

2.2   Seeing is believing

Michael Henderson was an eye witness to a hit and run accident. It was a dark night and the accident took place on a country road with no street lighting, but he said that he still had a good view of the car that killed the little boy. He is a willing witness. He can describe the car's make, colour, age and condition. He can even give a fairly good description of the driver's face and upper body. He is very certain and very credible as an eye witness. His professional background is as an expert scientist involved in DNA testing who has occasionally given expert evidence in court. He is a father with a child the same age as the child who was killed.

Michael is likely to be a credible, perhaps even unshakeable witness. It is less likely, given the lighting and the trauma of witnessing the death of a child, that his evidence will be as accurate as it is convincing. Studies report that many factors influence the perceptions of eye witnesses (Coon (1991)). The accuracy of visual perception can be impaired by poor lighting, stress and the attitudes and expectations of the observer. A confident witness or a professional observer (such as a police officer) is no more accurate than other observers (Coon (1991)).

We recognise people of our own race more accurately than others. The presence of a weapon impairs accurate recall of the face of the culprit. The longer we observe the scene, the more and the more accurately we are likely to recall it. In any event, we are likely to over-estimate the duration of dramatic events. Events recalled later might unconsciously incorporate information discovered in the meantime.

The perception of information through all the senses – sight, sound, smell taste and feel – follows more or less the same principles, although sight is the sense most studied. Some people have multi-sensual perceptions associated with sight. It is said that Sir Isaac Newton, for example (Vernon (1971)), associated red with the note C, orange with D, yellow with E, green with F, blue with G, and violet with B.

For most people, though, the unravelling of perceptions through one sense can be confusing enough. Test this out next time you taste several curries. Try and determine the spices present in some curries and absent in others.

The storing of memories through sight for later recall is a complex process. Sight perception will be influenced by lighting, distance from the event, colour, novelty, context and inferences about meaning both made by the observer and suggested by bystanders or later interrogators. Sight involves the recognition and storage of mental images in association with words and concepts. Paragraph 2.2.8 below sets out some tips on how to apply this information to routine legal work.

2.2.1 Some experiments in the limitations of visual perception

Some complexities of this process are revealed by recounting three famous experiments. In one experiment (Vernon (1971)), subjects were shown, for a short period of time, small line drawings that were both asymmetrical and irregular. Reproductions of the shapes by the subjects showed a tendency towards regularity and symmetry. In a similar experiment when drawings were given a name, the reproductions more closely resembled the name than the shape shown. Thus a figure depicting two circles of the same size sitting side by side and joined by a short horizontal line was reproduced as either spectacles or dumbbells depending on the language cue given to the observers.

The perception of colour can also be affected by ambiguity. In a famous experiment, observers were shown playing cards in which the colours were transposed. Hearts and diamonds were depicted as black, clubs and spades as red. Some people ignored the transposition entirely and reported seeing the cards as they should have been. Others recognised the differences. Some people transposed the colours to purple or grey, while a few people could not recognise them as playing cards at all (Vernon (1971)).

2.2.2   What we see depends on figure ground relationship

Consider Figure 2.1 below. If you take the dark portion as background, you will see a cup. If you take the light portion as background you will see two faces. Try and move from one to the other, so that you can 'see' both.

Figure 2.1

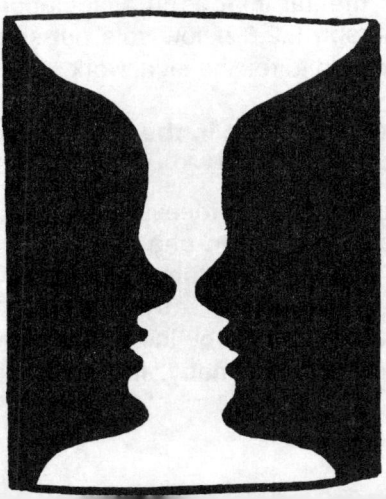

Necker's cube in Figure 2.2 works in the same way. Focus on the front of the cube, now focus on the back. The direction of the cube will vary depending on which facet you observe with greatest concentration, and which you take to be foreground and which you take to be the background.

Figure 2.2

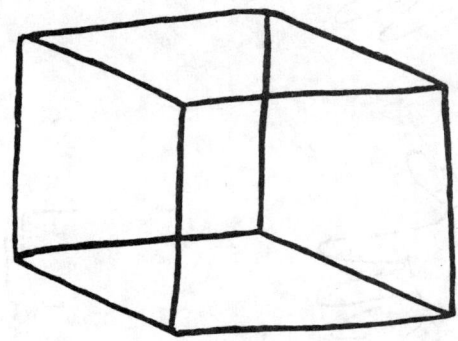

2.2.3   What we see depends on how we complete the outline

We see a figure in outline first and then fill in the detail. The less time we have to observe the object, the less detail we will actually record. The more familiar the object, however, the more we will try and resolve ambiguity. For example, look at the hands below in Figure 2.3 only for a second or two and then cover them. Does the palm face you or face away?

Figure 2.3

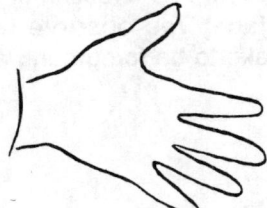
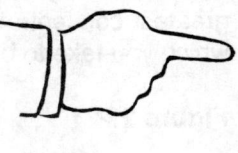

Figure 2.4a

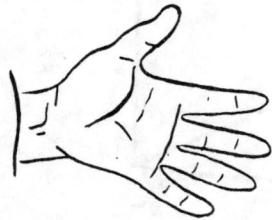

Actually, the question is not answered in the picture. You could complete it in your mind with the palm facing you, (Figure 2.4a) or the palm facing away (see Figure 2.4b). It might be the difference between a person examining his or her hand for skin lesions or raising a hand to slap you!

Figure 2.4b

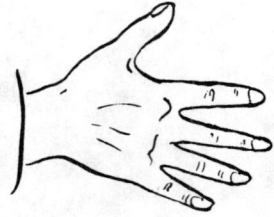
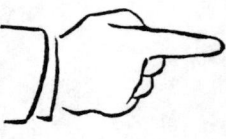

2.2.4   What we see is influenced by the surroundings

Consider the Müller-Lyer illusion in Figure 2.5 below. Which line is the longer, or are they both the same?

Figure 2.5

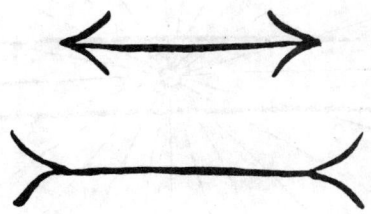

Likewise consider the T shape in Figure 2.6 below. Is the vertical line longer than the horizontal? Now measure them.

Figure 2.6

Consider the following shape in Figure 2.7 against the concentric circles. Trace the lines with a ruler and convince yourself they are straight!

Figure 2.7

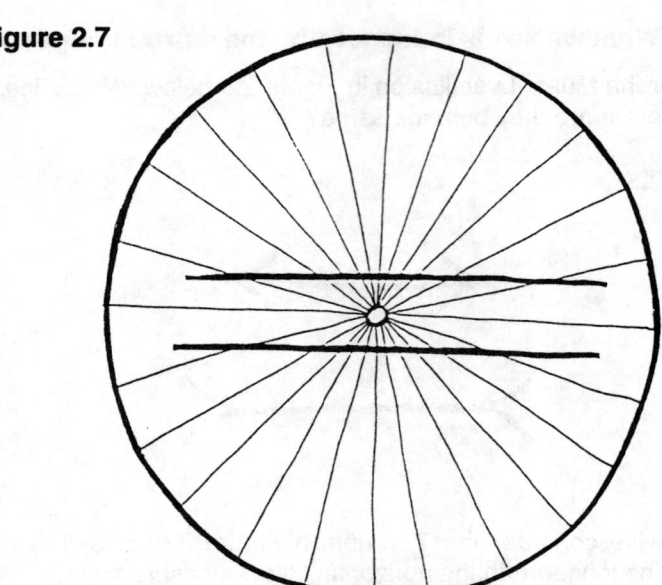

Which of the lines below run parallel in Figure 2.8?

Figure 2.8

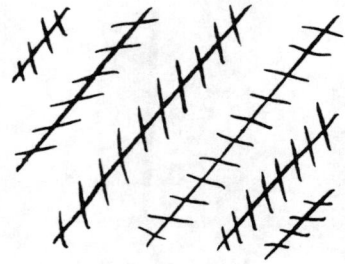

2.2.5   What we see depends on past learning

Consider the following phrase in the triangle in Figure 2.9. Find the repetition of the word 'the'. If you did not notice it, it might be because you have been conditioned both to expect that there will be no repetition of the definite article, and also that you were reading only the meaning words and not reading in proof mode.

Figure 2.9

Paris
in the
the spring

2.2.6   We will make what we see conform to that which is familiar, regular, symmetrical or complete

Look at the three pronged widget below in Figure 2.10. Your eye and brain will work hard to make sense of this image.

Figure 2.10

2.2.7   We tend to keep on seeing what we saw first

Once we have seen one thing, we tend not to look for further items in the picture.

Look at the rhomboid shape in Figure 2.11 below. You can see it as a chain of rectangles or as a kind of folded three dimensional shape. As a folded shape, you can see it like two roofs or like an upright Japanese screen. Chances are when you come back to this shape you will see the version you saw first. You will have to work really hard to see other versions, even after having captured them for a moment.

And so on. These are just examples of this fascinating field.

Figure 2.11

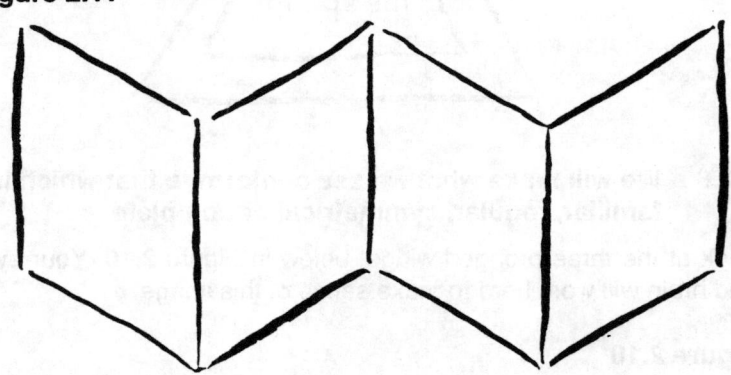

2.2.8   Lawyer's tips

As a lawyer relying on the perceptions of your own senses, you will be subject to these distortions. You should try to:

- perceive the same data on several occasions;
- ask the perceptions of others about the same data.

As a lawyer relying on witness perceptions you should:

- have the witness recall perceptions without interruption by you, or without collaboration with others;

- obtain independent evidence of time of day, lighting and atmospheric conditions;

- test the evidence of the other side's witnesses if necessary by conducting experiments under similar conditions;

- help the witness resist the tendency to perfect ambiguities or uncertainties in multiple recall. Ambiguity or uncertainty gives evidence greater force, because complete recall is rare.

2.3 Judgment under uncertainty – common failings

2.3.1 Narrative power versus abstract statistics

Margaret Henderson was an eyewitness to a traffic accident. Late one Saturday evening a taxi was involved in a serious accident in which a pedestrian was killed. There are only two types of taxi in this small town – blue and red. At that time 15% of the taxis on the road were blue, the rest were red. Margaret is adamant that the taxi involved in the accident was blue. The night was cloudy. She saw the taxi only after hearing the screeching of tyres. She was about 30 yards away. There were no street lights.

- What is the probability that Margaret is correct?

The court tested the reliability of the witness under the same atmospheric conditions as existed on the night of the accident and concluded that she identified one of the two colours correctly about 80% of the time.

- Will the jury believe Margaret?

If we take the advice of Bertrand Russell, we should predict that the jury will believe Margaret, even without evidence about her accuracy as a witness under the same atmospheric conditions. He said:

... popular induction depends on the emotional interest of the instances, not upon their number.

As a question of probability, the relatively small proportion of blue taxis on the road would make it much more probable that the taxi involved in the hit and run accident were red. Even given her accuracy under testing, it is still more probable that the taxi was red, since the base rate of red cabs on the road is higher than she is credible.

Kahneman, Slovic and Tversky (Kahneman, Slovic, Tversky (ed) (1982)) report the experiment upon which the Margaret Henderson story above is based, and many other interesting examples of experiments in which narrative material, even irrelevant material, influences the decision maker more than relevant underlying statistics (p 157). In the legal context, Posner (1990) observes that juries prefer causal rather than statistical explanations of events. Research constantly returns to the fact that thinkers are influenced more by the vivid single case, than by the representative facts.

In one experiment, reported in Kahneman (1982) (p 189), college students were asked to predict the behaviour of other college students in the following scenario. Six college students are discussing problems of adjusting to college life over headphones. Suddenly one of the students appears to suffer what sounds like a seizure. The students in the experiment are asked to predict the behaviour of the other five who listen to the seizure. They overestimated the number of people who would go to the victim's aid. They rated Greg R 'apathetic' for failing to go to the victim's aid, even when they were told that most people in the identical situation failed to aid the victim.

Researchers have concluded that people consistently overestimate the percentage of people who would behave as they do. They regard their own responses as appropriate. They also draw adverse inferences about those who would not behave as they would (Kahneman (1982) p 140).

This bears thought for judges who are in the position of assessing whether a criminal defendant, having behaved presumably in a way the judge would not behave, has breached the standard of the so-called 'reasonable' man or woman. It suggests that the judge is more likely to think that his or her behaviour reflects the standard, and that where the defendant's behaviour has deviated from that standard, the defendant's behaviour is amiss. It is assumed that the reasonable person behaves as would the silent majority. Sociological research in the United States at least, might suggest that the majority are less altruistic and more violent than the behaviour that we conceive as typical of the reasonable man or woman. The standard of the reasonable man or woman might actually be higher than that of the actual behaviour of the silent majority, and closer to the standard of behaviour of the Good Samaritan.

Vividness of particular memories accounts in part for what we concentrate on in reasoning. Other experiments produced equally intriguing results (citations to Kahneman (1982)):

- each spouse overestimated his or her own contribution to household chores, perhaps based on their greater knowledge of their own contribution (p 183);

- team members accounted for a loss in a game by remembering the failings of their own team members rather than the positive contributions of the members of the winning team (p 185);

- subjects remembered more vividly statements made by persons of another colour or race, rather than those from their own racial group.

2.3.2   The power of presentation

In a controlled experiment, subjects were presented with the following structures, A and B (Kahneman (1982) p 168).

A

x x x x x x x x

x x x x x x x x

x x x x x x x x

B

x x

x x

x x

x x

x x

x x

x x

x x

x x

They were told:

A path in a structure is a line that connects an element in the
top row to an element in the bottom row, and passes though
one and only one element in each row.

In which structure (A or B) do you think there are more paths?

How many paths do you think there are in each structure?

46 out of 54 subjects saw more paths in A than in B. You will
probably agree. Yet there are the same number of paths
($8^3 = 2^9 = 512$).

One might surmise why A seems to contain more paths. First,
there are three columns in A and only two in B. Paths in A are
shorter and therefore more easily visualised than paths in B.
Paths in B contain half the elements in the structure. Paths in A,
on the other hand contain only one eighth of the elements. I also
add that there might be a confusion of definition. The most

obvious paths in A that fit the definition are straight lines. Paths in B will consist of crooked lines which might have caused doubt about the definition of a line.

2.3.3   The order of presentation

In a further experiment, two groups of high school students were given five seconds to estimate the product of eight numbers.

Half were presented with the problem

8x7x6x5x4x3x2x1

Half were presented with the problem

1x2x3x4x5x6x7x8.

Research suggests that people attempt the first few operations and then estimate the product by adjustment. Since their adjustments are rarely sufficient, the same problem presented in a different order will yield radically different results.

In this experiment, both predictions were confirmed. The median estimate for the ascending sequence was 512. The median estimate for the descending sequence was 2,250. The correct answer is 40, 320 (Kahneman (1982) p 14).

2.3.4   More distortions in judgment

Other experiments reported in Kahneman suggest the following tentative conclusions:

1   The tenacity of the first view

Once people form a view about a subject, they fail to sufficiently adjust their view in the light of compelling information which contradicts it. So long as thinkers can articulate a persuasive case for their viewpoint, they will ignore contradictory evidence (Kahneman (1982) pp 144, 329).

2   Vividness of recall distorts judgment

The risks that people associate with certain events depend upon the vividness with which those events are recalled. They fear death by accident as much as death by disease, yet disease takes 16 times more lives. They fear plane travel more than car travel, even though death or accident by car is overwhelmingly more probable on a statistical basis. After a recent bush fire, they will be more concerned to insure against fire than theft, even though the background statistics suggest that theft is still more probable (Kahneman (1982) p 468). If they read through a list of people, they will judge that more men have been included in the list than women, if the famous people included in the list were men (Kahneman (1982) p 175).

3   Absence of significant data means it risks being overlooked

Sherlock Holmes observed that many people fail to take into account the evidentiary value of things which are missing or not done. Many detective stories present clues in the form of a slight change of behaviour in the murderer or the victim which the reader overlooks, but the hero or heroine does not. When presented with a diagnostic chart of reasons why a car might not start that omitted about half of the most common causes, people attributed causes only to those that were listed specifically. Those that were included only under the general heading 'Other problems' were effectively ignored. Even qualified mechanics were no better in recalling causes not mentioned specifically (Kahneman (1982) p 470).

4   Risk assessment can be affected by the way in which the risk is expressed

The probability of being injured or killed without wearing a seatbelt is much higher when the likely number of trips over a 50 year history is taken into account, than when expressed as the probability of accident occurring in a single trip. When considering a lifetime perspective, people considered the use of seat belts and air bags more favourably, than when the risks were expressed in terms of a single trip (Kahneman (1982) p 480).

5 Even with the benefit of hindsight there are distortions

Studies suggest that even in hindsight, people consistently exaggerate what should have been anticipated in foresight. They not only tend to view what happened as inevitable but also view it as having appeared 'relatively inevitable' before it happened. They judge that others should have been able to predict events better than is realistically likely or possible. They even misremember their own predictions, so as to exaggerate in hindsight what they knew in foresight (Kahneman (1982) p 341).

6 Problem solvers are often overconfident

Some research suggests that the confidence that the problem solver has that his or her own solution is correct often increases in ways which are not rational. Even professional problem solvers fail to learn from past mistakes. In studies as to how professional problem solvers calibrate future assessments to take into account past mistakes, only weather forecasters calibrated present decision-making sufficiently to take into account past mistakes; and only their level of confidence in prediction was factually related to the likelihood of being correct! (Kahneman (1982) p 431.)

2.3.5 Why distortions in judgment under uncertainty matter

These findings are relevant for lawyers in three ways. First, as thinkers we need to fight the tenacity of the first view, and the tendency to account insufficiently for subsequent data, by trying to see the problem in a new light whenever more data is revealed. Second, the distortions inherent in recall of past events and the tendency to attribute greater responsibility to people than situational factors might warrant, suggest avenues of enquiry for the lawyer that the client or witness is unlikely to suggest. Third, when counselling the client about the risk of trial, or the risks inherent in choices, for example, the lawyer will need to think carefully about how to frame the description of risk so that it is meaningful to the client.

The phenomena of overconfidence in judgment and selective reconstruction of past cases are not unknown in legal practice! The ability to predict how long a legal problem will take to solve, how much it might cost and what unanticipated delay factors might occur along the way is enhanced where the practitioner reviews past files on completion with a view to recalling how the decision factors changed along the way. Unfortunately, this is done only rarely. Complaints to the Law Society about solicitor delay in completing matters suggests that some lawyers consistently fail to educate their own clients' expectations about how long matters might take because, perhaps, they give insufficient thought themselves to the progress of past similar matters.

Distortions in judgment in uncertain situations are even more important when predicting the probability of future events.

2.4   Moving to probabilistic models of problem solving

The probabilistic model of decision-making is rarely taught in legal education. At law school we learn about predicting the decisions of courts in terms of predicting what the court should decide, based on an argument about what the law says and how it fits the facts. In non-litigious situations, we learn to read a legal text as a set of rules or principles and to apply the facts to them. This is a deterministic model.

In practice, however, advice will have elements both deterministic and probabilistic. We will first take a view of the law and how it applies to the given facts and then form a view about what a court should decide (the deterministic model). Closer to the trial, we will then move from determining what a court in abstract should decide to assessing the range of decisions likely from a particular court and relating those to financial loss or success for the client (the probabilistic model). In a non-litigious situation where the law is not clear-cut, clients will likewise make choices by assessing risk and benefit in a probabilistic way.

In designing processes for implementing legal solutions, we are also dealing with a probabilistic model. Too often we predict completion on the basis of the minimum time it should take, rather than building in a margin for inevitable delay or breakdown. The move from the first to the second model entails different problem-solving strategies that will be canvassed in subsequent chapters.

2.5   End of chapter references and additional reading

Coon, Dennis (1991)

Essentials of Psychology – Exploration & Application
West Publishing Co

Kahneman, Daniel
Slovic, Paul
Tversky, Amos (ed) (1982)

Judgment under uncertainty: Heuristics and biases
Cambridge University Press

Vernon, M D (1971)

The Psychology of Perception
Penguin

CHAPTER

3 The Lawyer Inside The Problem II

> 'A lawyer should be familiar with the skills and concepts involved in implementing a plan of action, including ... [a] realistic appraisal of one's own ability to competently carry out each of the aspects of the plan that should be handled by a lawyer ...'

The McCrate Report (1992)

> Lawyers 'just as much fun' as actuaries

Headline in *The Lawyer* Magazine (1993)

> Q.:Why have they started to use lawyers in laboratory experiments?
>
> A.:There are some things that rats just won't do.

Contemporary joke

The previous chapter looked at visual, perceptual and judgmental limitations that might imperil client, witness and lawyer.

This chapter looks at the role that personality preference might have in problem solving, focusing on the lawyer, but referring to communication between the lawyer, client and witness.

3.1 A metaphor

3.1.1 The individual and legal problem solving

We know the personality stereotype of the legal profession. The name of the lawyer in the cartoon *The Wizard of Id* says it all (Larceny E Pettifogger). He prefers to talk, not to act. When he acts, he does so reluctantly. His attention to detail is limited to mindless technicality aimed at catching out the other lawyer in the game of law. He places his own interests above client interest. On the rare occasion that he achieves something for the client, even he is surprised. Later the client discovers that the success cost too much, took too long and wasn't what he or she wanted anyway.

There are more measured comparisons of the behaviour of lawyers in comparison with the behaviour of other business people. In his book on the marketing of professional services, Wilson (1989) contrasts the professional interviewing style with the sales style. The professional sees interviewing as a process of information gathering, not of information sharing; of asking questions, not of answering them; of making statements, not of listening; of achieving credibility by demonstrating knowledge rather than by establishing trust. The lawyer in this professional context narrows the interview to that which he or she deems relevant. In contrast, the sales person opens up the interview trying to find out what the potential client thinks is relevant. With this legal style, small wonder that clients sometimes do not value the solution achieved for (not with) them.

3.1.2   Initial studies

The analysis of client complaints in the delivery of legal services has revealed some behavioural trends. The First Annual Report of the Solicitors Complaints Bureau (1988) observed that one quarter of all the 19,314 complaints received in 1987 related to delay or failure to reply to correspondence. Half of the complainants were lawyers. The errant practitioners compounded their own difficulties by treating the complaints from the Law Society with equal delay! (The Law Society of England and Wales' Guide to the Professional Conduct of Solicitors (1990).)

A recent study of indicative causes of claims in negligence against solicitors in the State of New South Wales, Australia, showed a high degree of correlation with causes reported by similar studies made by the American Bar Association, and the State of Oregon Bar. The NSW study by Streeton Consulting included follow-up interviews with 72 practitioners about 70 claims from 43 representative firms. The study identified three broad personality types which were each responsible for about one third of the negligence claims:

'Can Do'

The practitioner who is easy-going and eager to please; makes few file notes; writing few letters; weak on detail.

'Too Busy'

The practitioner who handles many files, works long hours and tries to process work efficiently by getting things done as quickly as possible.

'Usually Careful'

Although thorough and conscientious, this practitioner runs a personal system and fails to delegate

(Liverani (1993), North (1994)).

These are preliminary observations which require further consideration, rather than valid conclusions to be applied. If we could recognise a pattern we could facilitate future prediction and decision making. Much of legal practice involves predicting behaviour. Responsible professional practice also involves predicting one's own behaviour. Research about preferences reveals the potential avenues of investigation more fully.

3.2   Personality preference and valuing diversity

When Justin Evans joined Bligh, George and Smithers, a small but highly respected High Street law firm he was delighted. His first file on which he worked with Christopher George on a planning and environmental law matter was busy, stimulating, involving and exhausting. He loved it. The trouble started when he moved to the banking area to work with Jonathan Bligh. Everything Justin did seemed to be wrong. He preferred to discuss new matters with a partner to get a feel for what was required, but Jonathan said that was a waste of time and preferred to instruct via memo. Justin preferred to have all the files he was responsible for (and there weren't so many) ranged out on the desk in an untidy, although systematic, set of piles because they acted as a visual reminder. Jonathan insisted that he work with a clean desk and priority lists. In advice work, Justin preferred to speak to more experienced operators to get a sense of how far to research. Jonathan said that he must research the matter himself first. Justin preferred to make extensive hand-written notes before dictating a first draft. Jonathan said it was better to dictate as soon as possible and then revise it afterwards. Although Jonathan seemed satisfied with Justin's effort (he was never really pleased about anything), the stress of working against the grain was exhausting. Justin was very apprehensive about making a serious mistake.

We become so locked into our own way of getting things done that sometimes we forget that there are other routes to achieving an equally satisfactory result. We overestimate our own contribution and minimise that of others. We all have had the opportunity of working with people who are on the same wavelength as us, and, of working with those who are not. If we are not on the same wavelength as clients or supervisors, we can waste time and create stress working at cross purposes. The greatest danger in professional practice is that we assume that the other person will do certain things, while they are assuming that we will do them. Those things are never done at all.

Not only are lawyers stereotyped by clients, but we often stereotype our own colleagues – especially those unlike us in approach. Personality profiles provide a valuable aid for defining similarity and difference. Certainly they also present a stereotype. At least it is a richer, more varied and more valid stereotype than that which we each construct for ourselves. Personality profiles are used in business both for individual development and for developing more cohesive and effective teams. Three such approaches are described here:

- the Myers-Briggs Personality Type Inventory (MBTI);
- the Team Management Index;
- the Kolb Learning Styles Inventory.

Naturally, personality profiles have their limitations. They generalise across cultures. They need to be supplemented by information about (for example) background (social, ethnic, gender etc), values and achievements. They are only one of a number of possible tools which can assist us to understand ourselves and our colleagues better.

3.3   Myers-Briggs Personality Type Inventory

3.3.1   An overview

Katherine Cook Briggs and Isabel Briggs Myers developed the first such profile based on Jung's theory of personality generalised into four scales (the MBTI). Participants complete a paper test consisting of forced choice questions and paired words which, when scored, provides a profile from 16 possible personality types mapped onto a rectangular matrix. The profile indicates common preferences and enables participants to understand the ramifications of difference.

The profile produced by the MBTI reveals your preferences on four scales:

Extraversion versus introversion

This scale is about how you draw energy from the world. If you are an extravert, you will draw energy from other people. If you are an introvert, you will draw energy by concentrating on your own thoughts. Problem solving extraverts like to discuss ideas with others because they process information and make decisions while talking. Introverts, on the other hand, process information and make decisions by mulling issues over alone. (This description retains the Jungian spelling of extraversion.)

Sensing versus intuition

This scale is about how you direct your concentration. Sensers prefer to take in information through the five senses in the here and now. Sensers pay careful attention to the client's story and possible evidence. Intuitives are more attracted to following their hunches and by future possibilities. They are more likely to use a few key facts as a launching point for thinking.

Thinking versus feeling

This scale is about how you make decisions. Thinkers organise and structure information in order to make decisions analytically and objectively. Feelers make decisions in a more personal way oriented to their own values and feelings.

Judgment versus perception

This scale is described as how you prefer to live. Judgers have a preference for plan and order. Perceivers prefer a more spontaneous and flexible approach where they can in part make it up as they go along depending on how they feel (Hirsh and Kummerow (1990)).

3.3.2   Lawyers and MBTI

At a conference in 1992 on the United States, 3,014 practising attorneys were asked to complete the MBTI. Key findings reported about lawyers were (Richards (1993)):

Extraversion–introversion

This group of lawyers displayed a greater preference for introversion than the general US population, although within the group women displayed a more extravert preference than men.

Sensing–intuition

This group of lawyers displayed a greater preference for intuition – information which deals with possibilities and following through hunches – than the general US population who prefer facts and figures. This result is something of a surprise in terms of lawyers' common self perception as practical and objective. It might, in part, however account for the marked legal preference for abstract, not concrete, language.

Thinking–feeling

As against the general US population, this group of lawyers had a much stronger preference for deciding through structured, objective analysis, than on the basis of personal values.

Judging–perceiving

Likewise, a higher percentage of lawyers (61% men, 67% women) reported their preference for a planned and organised life as opposed to one which is more spontaneous and flexible.

The architectural configuration of most law offices supports this description of lawyers as preferring introversion, analysis and structure. Most law offices provide for individual offices for lawyers, but open plan for support staff. Cost of space in major cities forces lawyers to share small offices with one or two other lawyers, but they often observe that this is less than ideal. Lawyers say that confidentiality dictates this architectural choice. The few law firms which have moved to an open plan office arrangement feel that confidentiality is adequately covered by the use of conference rooms.

Of the 16 possible profiles, the lawyers in this study mapped into only four.

The concentration into four types suggests that client complaints about legal work might bring up issues and values alien to lawyers. Lawyers and law societies composed only of lawyers need to invite explanation and opinion about those complaints outside the legal profession in order to obtain a balanced view about their validity.

3.4   Team Management Index: linking personality preference with work roles

The questions in MBTI do not always specify the context – work or home – in which you are asked to describe your preferences. Both research (McCann (1990)) and personal experience suggest that in work situations we might have preferences which contrast with those felt at home. My own informal discussions about lawyer preferences reveal that lawyers who exhibit strong preferences for control, order, introversion and analytical thinking in the office find an outlet for flexibility, spontaneity, extraversion and their own beliefs in the selection of their hobbies or in the way they live at home.

The Team Management Index furnishes a profile that limits preferences to the work context and links them to the eight broad roles required in all work.

3.4.1   TMI Scales

Although the scales for the Team Management Index do not formally deal with all the same concepts as the MBTI (McCann (1990)), you will notice broad similarities with the MBTI scales already discussed. The four TMI scales are:

Extrovert–introvert

How you prefer to relate to other people. (TMI uses the now .conventional spelling for extrovert.)

Practical–creative

How you prefer to gather and use information. Practical people value and collect facts and figures, details of past successes and failures. They prefer answers to questions. They will often have no interest in making something which is already good better;

rather they see work as fixing or preventing problems. Creative people value diverse information, especially new ideas. They prefer questions and possibilities to answers. They love to be involved in making something already good even better.

Analytical–beliefs

How you prefer to make decisions. Analysts will gather and organise data in a systematic way and place great importance on logic, system and detail in decision-making. Because they see this technique as professional and objective, they are often unprepared for different views. People with a beliefs orientation, on the other hand, are strongly influenced by personal values in making decisions. They value the input of others into the decision-making process.

Structured–flexible

How you prefer to organise work. Highly structured people prefer to work with a detailed plan and dislike having to change the plan. Highly flexible people prefer to respond to the situation from time to time and are flexible on deadlines.

Work roles

TMI personality preferences map into eight main work roles ranged around a wheel. The names of the personality preferences are taken from the work roles they prefer. A personality is given one dominant and two related work role preferences. See Figure 3.1.

Figure 3.1

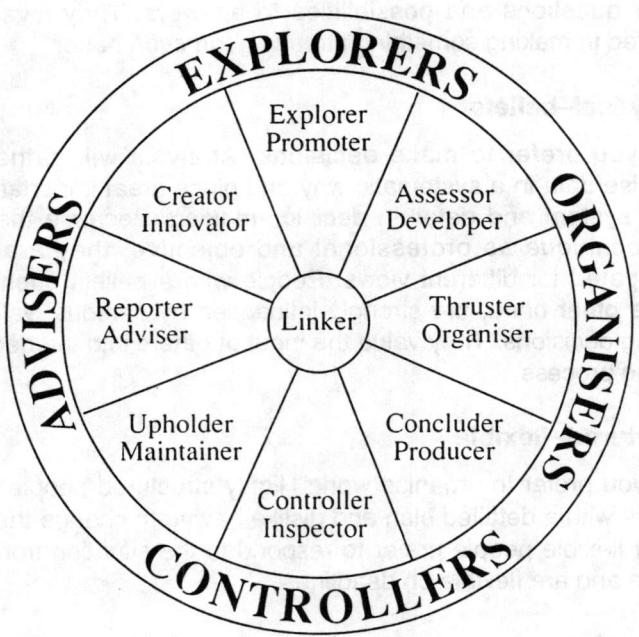

The dominant work role is determined by the participant's two
strongest preferences out of the eight listed above.

Explorers

Explorers record strong preferences for extroversion and creativity.

Their strengths are imagination especially visualisation and diagramming, a holistic approach incorporating other disciplines, experiences and insights, persuasiveness, optimism and future orientation.

Their weaknesses are often a lack of attention to detail, insufficient attention to what happened in the past, a lack of interest in the detail of implementation and maintenance. Their opposite type is Controller.

Figure 3.2a   The Explorer

Organisers

Organisers prefer analytical decision-making and structured work organisation.

Their strengths are their ability to move from thought to action, attention to practical detail within realistic constraints of time and cost.

Their weaknesses are sometimes a poor listening style and a tendency to move faster than the team might want without sharing information. Their opposite type is the Adviser.

Figure 3.2b   The Organiser

Controllers

Controllers record preferences for introversion and practical information gathering.

Their strengths are great attention to detail, constancy of purpose and ability to work to systems and deadlines.

Their weaknesses are lack of flexibility in work structure and sometimes low tolerance for difference in outlook or approaches, a focus on getting the present right rather than generating new services, skills or products for the future. Their opposite type is the Explorer.

Figure 3.2c   The Controller

Advisers

Prefer making decisions based on personal beliefs and are flexible in work organisation.

Their strengths are their ability to listen well including understanding underlying values and motivations, their strong adherence to ethical principles and fairness as they see it.

Their weaknesses are a preference to go on gathering information as opposed to deciding and acting. Their opposite type is the Organiser.

Figure 3.2d   The Adviser

3.4.2   Role preference and sensory perception

The early part of Chapter 2 dealt with some of the distortions inherent in visual perception for later recall. There is evidence to suggest that different personality types process information using the same senses in different ways and that particular personality types favour one of the sensory channels over others for information processing.

In fact, McCann (1988) suggests that most people select one mode from sight, sound, smell and feeling in order to perceive external reality. For example, in recalling a beach scene, one person might first associate the sight of the blue sea, another might recall the sound of the waves and the gulls, another might recall the smell of the salt or the oil slick, still another might remember the feeling of running on the hard sand with the sun burning on the skin.

In addition, McCann suggests that there are internal and external aspects to these preferences. Imagination is the internal aspect of the visual mode; accurate eye witness observation its external aspect. Strength in processing the internal mode will compete with accurate input from the external mode.

For illustration, I take two work roles in which this information is validated from my own experience of using TMI. The Explorer/Promoter, for example, has strong visual imagination. Any external visual information competes with what the Explorer/Promoter is conjuring up in the mind at the time of viewing. Explorer/Promoters are, therefore, often unobservant about detail and are often poor proof readers. The Thruster/Organiser, on the other hand, runs a strong internal auditory channel which means that events and conversations provoke an internal analytical dialogue with self. The Thruster/Organiser can be distracted by his or her own internal dialogue and literally not hear what is being said.

Careful observation of cues taken from the eyes, the cheeks and the colouration of skin, McCann observes, can give some clues

to the observer about the processing mode the speaker or listener
is accessing at the time. With practice, one can improve processing
in the weak channels and select the channels appropriate to the
listener, rather than those preferred by the speaker.

3.4.3   What role preference is common for lawyers?

Litigation lawyers and property lawyers often have an organising
or controlling preference Thruster/Organisers have a preference
for a business-like, action-oriented approach, with a focus on
pragmatic action. They dislike too much future-oriented chat
without a firm focus on action. If you are trying to establish rapport
with a Thruster/Organiser, you are advised to collect and marshal
your facts, contain your enthusiasm and present a rational,
succinct argument ending with who should do what.
Thruster/Organisers in a group often create a competitive
environment in which they enjoy playing devil's advocate and
creating mock power plays. Litigators of this personality type are
not natural mediators because of their relatively poor listening
skills.

McCann offers similar advice for establishing rapport and
working with each of the eight personality preferences (McCann
(1990)).

Data about lawyers collected so far reveals that the vast
majority map into the organising and controlling parts of the
wheel. The perceived slowness of the legal profession in
accepting change, much less initiating change, might be
accounted for, in part, by the relative absence of lawyers who
prefer the creative and explorer role (since these people like
change).

It is tempting to see a connection between:

*   rule-based approaches in jurisprudence and the world view of
    the introverted, structured analyst;

*   sceptical and pragmatic approaches and the world view of the
    person who is practical, flexible and analytical;

- sociological approaches and a personality which is extrovert, creative and makes decisions based on values.

Differences of approach are undoubtedly not so simple. But in living interaction between multiple problem solvers who find that they cannot co-operate easily, examination of role preference might assist understanding, if not agreement.

3.5   Learning style and problem solving

David A Kolb is an organisational psychologist. He postulates that both adult learning and problem solving are specialised examples of learning from experience. He further postulates that if the problem solver can start the problem solving process with a preferred activity, better solutions will result (Kolb (1984)).

He has identified four phases of this experiential learning process:

• concrete experience

This emphasises an unstructured and intuitive approach to problem solving focusing on people, valuing an open-minded approach.

• reflective observation

This emphasises careful and impartial observation looking for what is true or how things happen, seeking multiple perspectives and looking for implications.

• abstract conceptualisation

This emphasises the use of logic, ideas and concepts, trying to build theories and valuing precision and the cohesiveness of the system.

- **active experimentation**

This emphasises practical applications of knowledge involving influencing people and an assessment of what is likely to work, how to get things done, and valuing results.

Kolb theorises that the learning and problem solving process involves all four phases, but that most people will have preferences based on combinations of any two of the above four (mark your own here just for fun). He has developed a Learning Styles Inventory which can furnish you with this information. On this inventory, you might turn out to be:

- **A converger** – favouring abstract conceptualisation and active experimentation. People who prefer dealing with technical tasks rather than people problems; where a single correct answer is possible; where deductive reasoning is the primary logical mode.

- **A diverger** – favouring concrete experience and reflective observation. People who are people oriented with good intuitions and great imagination. They prefer open ended questions, where there is no correct answer where the generation of a number of possible solutions through sessions such as brainstorming is valued .

- **An assimilator** – favouring abstract conceptualisation and reflective observation. People who want a theory to be sound, rather than practical; who are more concerned with ideas and concepts than people; where their capacity for reflection enables them to produce models or explanations for disparate data through inductive reasoning .

- **An accommodator** – favouring concrete experience and active experimentation. People who are happy to act in an uncertain world and will carry out tasks where the structure or outcome is not clear. They will rely on other people for information rather than their own analysis. They solve problems intuitively on a trial and error basis.

My own experience with commercial lawyers suggests that in any group, there will be only one or two divergers and a few accommodators. The majority of the group will be either assimilators and convergers. Convergers and assimilators are often uncomfortable delegating research on a problem, since they emphasise analysis of fact and law in reaching a solution. They are likely to research a point first and ask the opinions of others later. The accommodator and the diverger, on the other hand, are more likely to ask opinions of others first in order to channel their research more efficiently later.

The Kolb Learning Styles Inventory can be useful for helping lawyers understand that different approaches to researching and completing a problem in their own team are equally valid. These approaches might amount to no greater difference than a different order in which the same tasks are carried out.

3.6   From the problem solver to problem solving

None of the systems discussed would aim to provide a complete picture of any person profiled. The profiles do not report on knowledge, intelligence, skill or experience. However, they each reveal differences in areas that can cause conflict in work. An understanding of similarity and difference can improve a co-operative process of problem solving, reducing time wasted and improving results.

Having looked at processes of thinking, perception, and conception internal to the problem solver (and the client), we can now move to a consideration of the stages through which the solution is processed from presentation of the problem to implementation of the solution.

3.7   End of chapter references and additional reading

Hirsh, Sandra   *Introduction to Type in*
Kummerow, Jean   *Organisations*
(1990)   Australian Psychologists Press, Carlton

Kolb, David A
Rubin, Irwin M
McIntyre, James M
(1984)

Organisational Psychology
Prentice Hall Inc, USA

Liverani, Mary Anne
(1993)

*Risk Management Offers to Reduce
Claims and Make Happier Clients*
NSW Law Society Journal p 32

Margerison, Charles
McCann, Dick
(1990)

Team Management
Mercury, London

McCann, Dick
(1988)

How to Influence People at Work
Heinemann Professional
Publishing

North, Ronwyn
North, Peter
(1994)

*Managing Client Expectation and
Professional Risk*
Streeton Consulting

The Law Society
(1990)

*The Guide to the Professional Conduct of
Solicitors*
UK

Wilson, Aubrey
(1989)

Marketing of Professional Services
McGraw Hill, USA

CHAPTER

4 Back To A Model For Legal Problem Solving

'All professions are conspiracies against the laity.'

George Bernard Shaw

4.1   Why a model?

If the legal profession is a conspiracy against the laity, the conspiracy is not very efficient. Lawyers rarely share common approaches to problem solving. As we have seen, that might be accounted for in part by differences in perception, thinking style and personality.

In order to learn, to develop and to hone any process, the learner builds a model of the process in his or her mind so that mistakes will be remembered and not repeated and so that successful approaches, knowledge or techniques can be applied in the future. A shared model valid for, or adaptable to, many situations would facilitate discussion about the problem solving process between professionals. The model would contain a shared understanding of both process and content. A problem solving model would be used to integrate the approaches of all personality types – from the Explorer/Promoter's focus on the big picture, to the Controller/Inspector's insistence on detail. The use of a complete model could act:

- as a checklist for all the categories of relevant risk factors a lawyer needs to avoid;

- as a directing device for structuring problem solving so that lawyers do not get drawn into one aspect of the problem solving process (perhaps by personal preference), and forget about other aspects;

- as a checklist of choice for thinking, communicating and acting so that all possible choices are considered.

4.2   Some general models of problem solving

Few such models have been attempted for legal problem solving.
The process is more developed in management and psychology,
so I start with some samples of these problem solving models.
Some of the models are in the form of text only, some include
both text and diagrams.

4.2.1   Problem solving as action

A simple problem solving model used in business is used to focus
thinking on desirable change and means of achieving it. It is a
kind of means-end analysis, a long borrowing from Machiavelli.

One asks:

- Where are we now?
- Where do we want to be?
- How can we get there?

Where are we now?

This involves a description of the current state of affairs including
characterising the organisation, resources and profitability,
comparing it with competitors, isolating factors to remain and
those to change, evaluating resources and strengths and
weaknesses. A SWOT analysis is also helpful – looking at
strengths, weakness, opportunities and threats.

Where do we want to be?

In business this might be a one line answer, for example, a desire
to increase dividends to shareholders. It can also involve a
detailed vision of change – if an organisation, one might
characterise the number, educational level and skill base, gender
and other mix of staff; visualise the work environment and location
by size, location, external appearance and internal layout; identify
the industries, products and services to be produced. The greater
the detail, the easier the next stage.

How do we get there?

The richer the vision of where we might want to be, the easier it is to work out how to get there. This is the action stage specifying a plan for action and the actors; perhaps outlining contingency plans, or identifying critical points for refining or reassessing the vision along the way.

A focus on action and driving events through time is appropriate where the goals are fairly easily defined and most of the difficulties will be in the implementation. As a matter of motivation, it allows input by everyone involved in the vision of the end result. That vision can motivate during the difficulties of the implementation phase. This approach also places a high premium on planning skills.

This approach might be useful for lawyers when planning and writing letters of advice. A lawyer's letter usually gives most space to analysis and less space to implementation. The provision of a timetable and a checklist, in addition to advice would correct the balance.

Where legal problems are really messy, it is even harder to decide what to do. Those problems might benefit from an approach which allows more focus on generating different versions of possible problems, possible solutions and possible means of implementation – the creative approach.

4.2.2 Problem solving as creation

Creativity is a quality most associated with artists, novelists, painters, composers, or with scientists such as Archimedes, Einstein or Mandelbrot. The study of how these people create, reveals how techniques of creative thinking can be adapted to find solutions to humble everyday problems. In the world of commerce and law, creative thinking need not be a revolution. Chaos theory suggests that small changes made at the beginning of a system can have huge effects. Creative thinking in law might involve either a borrowing from another discipline, or a small change in the normal legal way of doing things.

Graham Wallas identified the following five stages in creative thought (Wallas (1926); Coon (1991)).

Orientation (sometimes described as **Interest**) in which the problem or issue is defined and achieves some focus.

Preparation in which the thinkers saturate themselves in as much relevant information as possible.

Incubation in which thinkers do something else so long as the problem resists solution. This is when the subconscious works on the problem.

Illumination (often described as the AHA! Experience) in which the thinker often *sees* the answer and greets it like an old friend.

Verification in which the answer must be validated, usually by applying direct analytical thinking in the conscious mind.

We all have had the experience of coming to the solution before the reasons. Indeed, it is sometimes asserted that judges often first come to a decision and later find the reasons for that decision when writing a judgment. Lawyers are fortunate that their mode of working is particularly conducive to the illumination phase, since they tend to work on more than one file at once, often over long periods of time. Ideas from one file can be processed in the subconscious to help decisions on another file. Lawyers are probably less likely to utilise the orientation and preparation phases as effectively as they might; partly because clients often do not see lawyers as solving problems but merely as recording answers, with the result that there is little time for saturation.

The essence of the creative process seems to be an interchange between the stress of looking at the problem hard and close and then the release of stress by doing something else.

Unsticking or *unblocking* the problem solver is also one of the other elements of creative problem solving. Looking at a problem closely and especially under pressure can mean that the problem solver develops a block about the problem beyond which he or she seems not to be able to progress.

Our problem solving model should borrow some features of the creative process which appear to be helpful when the thinker gets stuck.

Creativity when you are stuck (I)

You can experience the process of being unstuck right now. Each picture below represents a well known legal expression. You can discover the legal expression, even if it is not personally familiar to you, by saying exactly what you see. Think of it as a kind of visual onomatopoeia. Try this first one (Figure 4.1)

Figure 4.1

Yes! You got it! Solicitor on the record.

Now try these. The answers are at the end of this chapter.

Figure 4.2a

Figure 4.2b

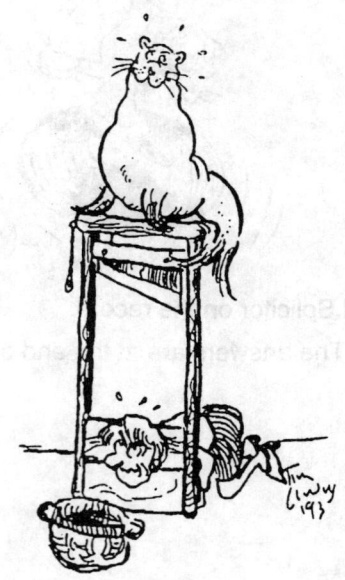

Figure 4.2c

Figure 4.2d

Figure 4.2e

Figure 4.2f

Chances are that some of the answers just popped into your mind without any conscious thought. Chances are that you solved them in random order. Chances are that the ones where *you* were stuck were not the same as the ones that frustrated *others* who were reading the book at the same time. The point is, once you discovered the answers to a couple of these, you could work the answers to the others out analytically by comparing the answers to the easy ones and hence discovering the process.

We need to learn when to focus closely on a problem and when to relax. Certain phases of the problem solving process require expansionary thinking, to enable the listing of as many possibilities as possible. Certain phases of the problem solving process require contractionary thinking, to enable selecting and prioritising.

Creativity when you are stuck (II)

The expansionary and the contractionary thinking modes are opposites. Some people are better at expansionary thinking. Others are better at contractionary thinking. Both are modes which can be taught and learned. Alex Osborn, in his book *Applied Imagination*, suggests that there are a number of unblocking activities that can be fruitful: they are listed below. They are all examples of expansionary thinking.

Adapt

Ask:

How have other people solved this problem in the past? What can I adapt, modify or copy?

Magnify or minimise

Ask:

What would I do if I made this problem bigger or smaller or if I have all the time in the world or only had until lunchtime?

Rearrange

Ask:

How can I reorganise the facts, the law, the objectives, to see the problem anew, for example, look at cause and effect, move from objectives back to means, start at a different point in the chronology, look at it from another person's point of view?

Reverse

Ask:

Can I look at it from the other lawyer or other side's point of view?

Combine

Ask:

What happens if I mix elements of this problem with some other problem?

It is unlikely that creativity in law will require discovering an equivalent to the theory of relativity. Creativity in law might mean:

- adopting the creative process when you are stuck;
- adopting some creative thinking techniques to increase the list of options upon which you then exercise rational thinking.

You will be given practice in both expansionary and contractionary modes of thinking in Chapters 5 to 8.

4.2.3 Problem solving with hats and shoes

Edward de Bono (1985) has produced two metaphors for thinking and action that incorporate both rational problem solving and creative approaches. Six coloured hats enable one person, irrespective of personality preference, to view a problem from multiple perspectives. The advantage of a hat is that it can be worn and removed, so that the choice of thought process becomes a deliberate selection of tools. The hats enable the thinker to try out the roles for effectiveness without having to adopt the underlying values.

The hats are:

White for facts and figures;

Red for emotions, intuitions and feelings;

Black for speculating about what might be wrong or incorrect;

Yellow for speculating about what might be right, positive and constructive;

Green for generating lateral and creative ideas and approaches;

Blue for designing a thinking scheme in which the hat colours are consciously selected.

This means that a thinker can look optimistically at a situation by wearing a yellow hat without having to be an optimist, or can look critically for error by wearing a black hat without actually being a pessimist. You can tell others the approach you are adopting from time to time by saying something like 'Let's do some green hat thinking', or 'Let's now subject these ideas to the black hat.'

De Bono has devised a similar process for action by using the metaphor of shoes. To act, one chooses from six pairs of shoes which can be worn in a matched pair or in combination.

The shoes are:

Navy formal shoes for routines and procedures;

Grey sneakers for investigation of facts;

Brown brogues for pragmatic effective action;

Orange gumboots for everyday situations involving risk and requiring a solution specially designed;

Pink slippers for caring;

Purple riding boots   for adoption of action within a formal role, for example, as a judge.

There is no controlling pair of shoes analogous to the blue hat because shoes have the added advantage that they can be worn in combination. A litigious transaction, for example, would involve a grey sneaker for the facts coupled with a navy formal shoe to initiate the usual proceedings. Closer to settlement, one would combine a brown brogue for pragmatism but keep an orange gumboot for that special variation or emergency. The advocate would don the purple riding boots for the trial.

The hats and shoes approaches assume that, with practice, practitioners can broaden their repertoire of approaches, irrespective of their personality preferences. Depending on the strength of personality preferences , the approaches required by some hats and shoes may be so foreign that a problem solver might need a lot of practice, and assistance, to be able to use them effectively.

4.2.4   Problem solving as learning

The previous chapter dealt with Kolb's Learning Styles Inventory that identifies the participants preferred behaviour for learning. The four learning phases are reflected in Kolb's Model of the four phases of problem solving. They are *phases* because problem solving is notionally a four step process, in its most abstracted form, taking place in the following order:

- situation analysis (involving concrete experience);

- problem analysis (involving reflective observation);

- solution analysis (involving abstract conceptualisation);

- implementation analysis (involving active experimentation).

Note that the problem solver can enter the process at any of these four stages, but to view the problem adequately from all sides, he or she should then proceed in the sequence (above) through the other three.

Within each of the four stages, there will be a stage in which the mind *expands* possibilities using the more creative thinking approaches listed above (para 4.2.2) and then *contracts* them using the more analytical and rule-based approaches yet to be discussed. Kolb calls the expansionary processes *the green mode mind set* and the contracting approaches *the red mode mind set*. The full model appears at Figure 4.3 (Kolb (1984)).

Figure 4.3

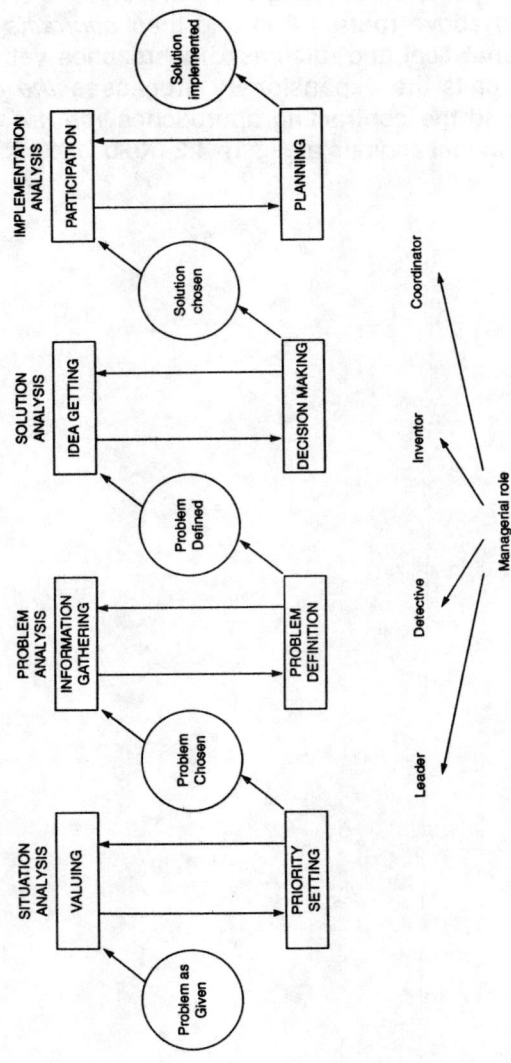

Kolb/Rubin/Mcintbyre Organisational Psychology: An Experiential Approach to Organisational Behaviour, © 1984, p. 156. Reprinted by permission of Prentice-Hall, Inc., Englewood Cliffs, NJ, USA

This is, of course, an idealised process. It is the rare problem solver, even a lawyer, who solves problems by following through Kolb's stages in such an orderly way. For example, although it is logical to start at situation analysis showing the virtues of open-minded reflective observation, thoughts occur to the problem solver in a random way, often in accordance with the thinker's relative values about and interest in reflective observation, gathering multiple perspectives, practical results orientation and theoretical soundness.

4.2.5   The model of reflective practice

Donald Schon has drawn attention to the need to extend the education of professionals beyond instruction in the rules, principles and concepts that are believed to determine solutions to client problems. He recommends that all trainee professionals perform professional work under conditions in which the learner can engage in reflective dialogue with a more senior practitioner. His call for the *reflective practicum* echoes the phase of reflective observation in Kolb. This moment to moment feature of problem solving relating to real life *messes* is absent from the university education of most professionals.

The reflective practicum is Schon's answer to the dilemma that not all professional thinking can be neatly reduced to rules, principles, concepts models or charts. The reflective practicum reveals the senior professional's thought processes to the learner from moment to moment.

In the context of modelling problem solving in engineering, Blockley (1992) has developed a model of problem solving viewed as a looped psychological process based on Schon's idea of reflective practice. The problem solver perceives the world, reflects upon the world in the light of the problem or the possible solutions or both, acts in some way and then perceives the world anew in the light of those conceptions and actions. Reflection is a process of triggering memory, using imagination to devise possibilities, devising scenarios of ordered sequences of possible action, and evaluating the memories, possibilities, and scenarios. This cycle of reflection is similar to the phased process identified by Kolb.

Blockley further enriches his conception of the problem solving process by conceiving of it as *a hierarchically structured set of evolutionary problem-solving processes* with many levels of definition. The patterning devised by the interaction between perception, reflection and action is depicted at Figure 4.4.

Figure 4.4

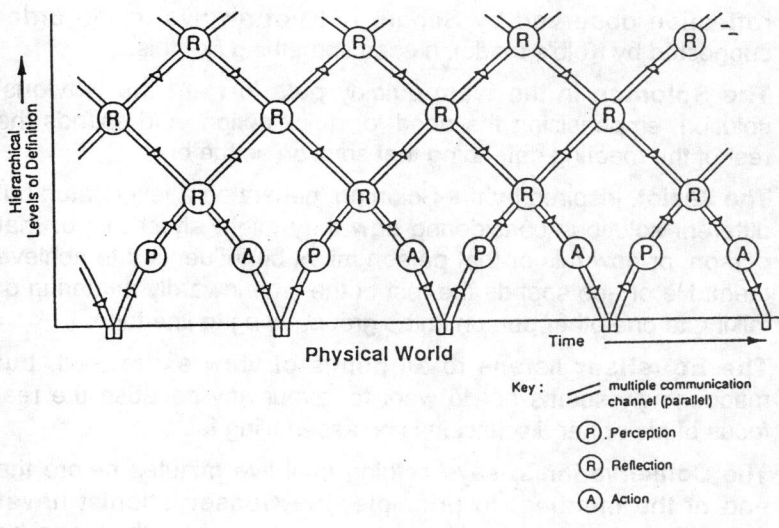

I have too little space to do real justice to the insight and elegance of Blockley's design. Suffice it to say that as a picture of problem solving, it is more compelling than the orderly phased models because it approximates both the mess and the order which we experience as problem solvers. Most problem solvers actually process several phases of problem solving simultaneously – the mind fluttering between situation analysis, problem analysis, option identification and possibilities for implementation. Perceptions about each phase feed into conceptions about the other phases in a structure more like Blockley's hierarchical web and less like Kolb's phased approach.

4.2.5   Lawyers problem solving as professional artistry

My own experience of lawyers solving a problem in groups is that there is a sort of phased process at work involving the debate and reflection observed by Schon, but not always in the order suggested by Kolb's model. It goes something like this:

The Solomon in the team quickly puts forward the 'obvious' solution, emphasising the need for quick action, and spends the rest of the meeting defending that solution as the best.

The Zealot, inspired by the Solomon, generates a few related but different solutions considering how they might affect this or that person, or how this or that person might be influenced to achieve them. He or she spends the rest of the time inwardly muttering or talking to one other person in the group, trying to fine tune.

The Equaliser listens to all points of view expressed, but maddeningly seems not to want to favour any because the real focus of his or her discussion is on assembling facts.

The Conservationist says nothing until five minutes before the end of the meeting. In principle, the Conservationist never expends more emotional energy on a problem than can be helped. Almost at the end of the meeting, the Conservationist points out dryly that they have all made invalid assumptions and therefore answered the wrong question. In any event, a similar matter has just been completed by someone else in the firm and all they need to do is get that person involved or borrow his or her file as a precedent!

At this point, with three minutes to go, the group of lawyers then prepare an agenda for the next meeting which looks at the facts, law, possible solutions and means of implementation in a more systematic way.

At this stage, adopting Kolb's model, and learning to value the approaches of other learning styles, would have many advantages for lawyers who solve problems like this.

The Solomon and the Zealot would learn that a little more time spent on reflective observation at the situation appraisal phase will always yield a longer list of things which could be done, rather than just the obvious solution. Greater consultation with others better at processing detail would help them avoid mistaken characterisations of the legal problem which waste time.

The Equaliser should be favoured in analysis of all the facts. **The Solomon** and **the Zealot** can offset the indecisiveness sometimes shown by **the Equaliser**.

The Conservationist would insist that the others process the questions systematically, to avoid wasting time discussing action before the facts are complete or before the problem is properly characterised.

The personality preferences of the problem solver are built into Kolb's model. The problem solver with a tendency to focus on one phase only can be reminded of the approaches to problem analysis and solution that are also needed. The lawyer's orientation for rules, analysis and action, can be supplemented by a conscious search for people who see solutions in terms of people, possibilities and ideas. Where all personality types are not present on the problem solving team, the hats and shoes tools developed by de Bono can remind the team of approaches that might be absent from the group and that can be applied systematically.

Following a common process consciously becomes more important as lawyers increasingly work in teams with a range of different specialisms. It will become even more important as lawyers work more with other professions ie management consultants, architects and accountants, who are more used to a self-consciously, planned approach. The Kolb model has the advantage of merging the creative approach to problem solving with the more traditional, rule-based analytical approach.

Approaches to modelling legal problem solving have many similarities with the models set out thus far.

4.3   Some models for legal problem solving

In 1991, The American Bar Association issued a tentative draft
(ABA (1991)) which later became a full report, the McCrate Report
(ABA (1992)) setting out the fundamental skills and professional
values underlying the practice of law as part of its examination
into how to narrow the gap between law school and practice (see
para 4.3.4). In the course of the ABA work, numerous articles
were reviewed that evaluated whether law school teaches
students how to think like a lawyer. This quotation from Gee and
Jackson (1977) summarises the core of the argument:

> ... If legal educators were to agree on anything it is that legal
> analysis is taught in law schools. It is usually taught indirectly,
> that is, as a by-product of the case book method. The process
> of legal analysis is treated as a gestalt with components
> remaining unexpressed beyond the ultimately tautological
> observation that one applies the law to the facts. As a result,
> there is no shared articulated model of legal analysis. Each
> professional develops his (sic) own consciously or
> unconsciously. The models, therefore ... are idiosyncratic ...

This article confirms that the model building is not part of the
legal conspiracy – it is left largely to the individual. Yet in spite of
this highly individualistic approach, some lawyers have
succeeded in developing generic models for legal problem
solving. The following models of problem solving are discussed
below:

- The Phased Model
- The Means End Model
- The Predictive Model
- The Complete Professional Model

4.3.1   The Phased Model

Both of the models discussed under this heading are called
Phased Models because they emphasise content to be thought

about through time.

Jackling and his co-authors produced the following algorithm describing the process of solving legal problems. It recognises that the thinker might need to run through the whole process a number of times before the problem is solved. It also sees that the process involves a series of phases which can be abstracted into a more or less chronological process. See Figure 4.6.

Figure 4.6

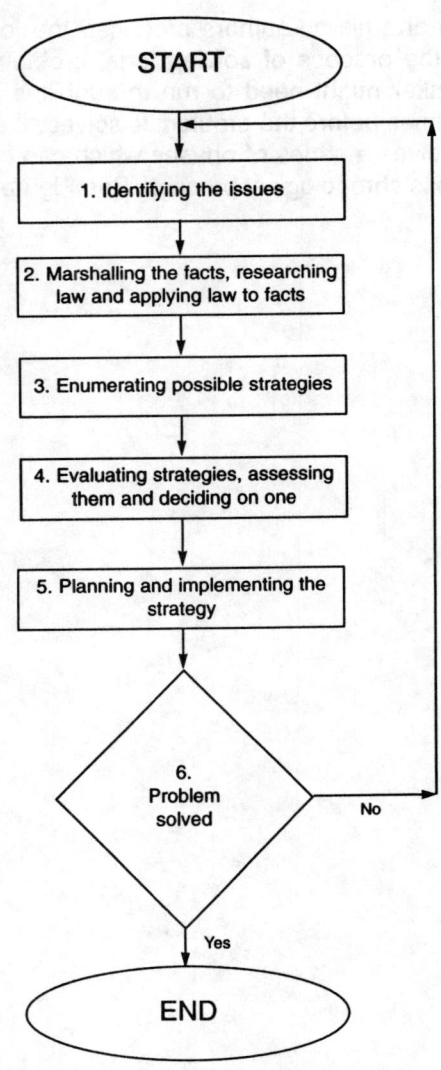

Jackling, Lewis, Brandt and Sell (1990)

Nathanson (1989) has produced a similar model, also viewing problem solving as a five phase process notionally ordered as follows:

- problem and goal identification;
- fact-investigation;
- legal-issue identification and assessment;
- option identification and decision-making;
- planning and implementation;

Nathanson argues for problem solving as the unifying theme in legal learning and legal work. He also specifies the use of a model as a useful tool for helping the student or practitioner transfer learning from one law subject or legal file to another.

A slightly more detailed Phased Model is to be found in Twining and Miers (1991).

Adapted from non-legal problem solving, Twining and Miers describe phases as::

- clarification of the actor's standpoint-role, objectives and general position;
- perception of 'facts';
- evaluation of one or more of the elements as mischievous, undesirable or an presenting an obstacle to the attainment of some objective;
- identification of a range of possible courses of action;
- prediction of likely obstacles and costs associated with each possible course of action;
- choice of general policy and means;
- implementation of the choice (my paraphrase).

This last Phased Model introduces the specific elements of role and standpoint, as well as means, ends and costs so often vital in practice.

4.3.2   The Means End Model

Anthony G Amsterdam (1984) has observed that there are possibly only three kinds of analytic thinking taught in traditional law schools:

*   case reading and interpretation;
*   doctrinal analysis and application;
*   logical conceptualisation and criticism.

He goes on to suggest that perhaps a total of only seven kinds of reasoning are taught in any law school against the 15 or 20 kinds of reasoning which might be used in legal practice.

One of the types of reasoning not taught is means-end analysis. Amsterdam identifies its relevance to problems to be solved or opportunities to be capitalised upon. Means-end analysis looks similar to the problem solving as action model set out at the beginning of this chapter.

To perform means-end analysis, one must:

*   canvass all possible goals thoroughly, creatively and systematically;
*   make an inventory of all the possible means to achieve each of the goals, including making a strategic assessment of issues such as the importance of keeping as many goals and means open for as long as possible;
*   assess the means to determine;

    (i)   which means are compatible or incompatible with which goals

    (ii) which incompatibilities can be reconciled

    (iii) a basis for prioritising means.

Amsterdam adds that the analysis might include prognosticating a best case/worst case scenario for each of the means. One will need to assess, rank, prioritise and cost goals as well as means. Posner likens means-end analysis to economic risk-benefit analysis (1990).

Many commentators make the point that this is one possible approach judges use in writing judgments; they come to the conclusion first and then later use authority to explain and validate the conclusion already conceived. Means-end analysis is a common approach for a commercial lawyers whose practice aims to help clients structure their affairs for the future in the most risk-free and most efficient way.

This approach does not exclude the issues highlighted for consideration in the Phased Model; rather it recasts the problem as a question of directly listing what should or could be done and on what basis. In the Phased Model action is a by-product inferred from an analysis of the law.

4.3.3 The Predictive Model

This approach might perhaps be more correctly characterised as a theory rather than a model (Posner (1990)). Sometimes the success of a lawyer as problem solver will require the lawyer to predict successfully the decision of a court or tribunal. In these situations, the lawyer will move the focus away from his or her own case facts and law and will look at previous decisions on similar facts in the recent past, including preferences (even biases) of the individuals presiding or inherent to the jurisdiction. A personalised predictive model is used by barristers practising in the personal injuries area who are very familiar with awards made by judges and juries for similar claims in the recent past. They are also aware of differing attitudes of different presiding officers to the same case.

The Predictive Model is not a complete model for a whole transaction. It is an approximate heuristic helpful to the decision of whether to settle or whether to go to court. In recent years, computer models developed to process complex decisions using probability theory have been adapted for use in more complex legal settlements.

4.3.4   The Complete Professional Model

The Task Force on Law Schools and the Profession (ABA (1992)) ('the McCrate Report') identified 10 skills and four values involved in legal practice. They are as follows:

Skills

1   Problem solving
2   Legal analysis and reasoning
3   Legal research
4   Factual investigation
5   Communication
6   Counselling
7   Negotiation
8   Litigation and alternative dispute resolution procedures
9   Organisation and management of legal work
10 Recognising and resolving ethical dilemmas

Values

1   Provision of competent representation
2   Striving to promote justice, fairness and morality
3   Striving to improve the profession
4   Professional self-development

Problem solving is a five step model summarised here, but which is outlined in much more detail in the McCrate Report.

- Identifying and diagnosing the problem including noting the client's situation and problem, the client's goals, supposed and preferred courses of action and financial resources, limits to what is known including the cost of discovering more and the time line for resolution.

- Generating alternative solutions and strategies which are independent, systematic and creative, noting possible limitations on this analysis by identifying assumptions, gaps, and assertions of doubtful evidentiary value.

- Developing a plan of action including listing possibilities ranking them, and settling upon one.

- Implementing the plan including assessing whether the given lawyer is the appropriate person to do so.

- Keeping the planning process open to new information and ideas.

This is a more content-filled model than the others considered so far. Problem solving refers to most of the skills and incorporates three out of the four values. It is an action model and may serve as a reminder list of all the heads of action that might be taken. It may as a consequence seem to de-emphasise situation and problem analysis.

In its draft form, the description of problem solving lacked sufficient reference to consultation with the client and educating the client's expectations. This has been remedied in the final report.

The listing of all 10 skills and all four values probably contains all the headings which a useful problem-solving model would need to contain, but they are not arranged in a way which would be accessible to the practitioner at the desk.

In discussing the model, the McCrate Report emphasises using means-end analysis as a tool; the importance of creativity, sound judgment and personal insight as prime attributes of the legal problem solver; and independence as an essential feature of the context of problem solving for lawyers.

4.4 The elements of a useful model for legal problem solving

There is always tension between simplicity and completeness in model building. The model needs to be simple enough to be memorable, at a sufficiently high level of generality to be relevant, but needs to adequately focus all the categories that the problem solver should address including mistakes to avoid.

A rich model would use all the senses and engage all parts of the brain through colour, text, pictures, and diagrams. A really rich model would use sound and light to move through time rather like an animation to emphasise the dynamic nature of the process itself.

We have the basis of such a model from those already described. Many of the models share common descriptions of the phases of problem solving as a four or five step process. In a law school problem, the linear direction of the Phased Model faithfully reproduces the conscious steps taken to think about the problem. In a real-life problem, the dual thinking activities of expansion and contraction at each of the phases from the Kolb model are a useful addition, as is the webbed complexity of the mind shuttling between the phases from the Blockley model.

None of the models includes a specific list of things to avoid as determined by claims in negligence against the private practising profession. As a model for use in practice, this could be a helpful feature. The Law Society of England and Wales has produced such reminders on single laminated cards – a warning about fraudulent property schemes and a reminder set of issues in giving undertakings. They are even colour coded!

Only the Professional Model specifically recognises that legal problem solving takes place within an organisational context which might impose constraints on the problem solver – the firm might have a policy not to do certain work; might be constrained because of a retainer or doing defendants' only work; might have a certain philosophical stance or policy about pro bono work.

Only the Kolb model links the issue of personality preference with problem solving. And finally, only the Kolb Model permits the thinker to start at any point in the process.

4.5   Elements peculiar to legal problem solving

Legal problem solving also has some peculiar features that a model designer needs to take into account.

1   Lawyers describe looking up the law as *research* when what they usually do is more properly called *search*. Research in other disciplines means forming a hypothesis and testing it, including researching analogous approaches in other disciplines. Having learned *search*, lawyers often do not learn *research*. The model should fill this gap.

2   Lawyers have their own ethical rules which constrain behaviour and which sometimes confer advantage. The rules relating to confidentiality and conflict of interest are examples of how lawyers' behaviour can be constrained. The doctrine of professional privilege is an example of rules conferring advantage.

3   Even in the parts of legal practice that are highly regulated and codified the lawyer might have to furnish a text for the rule inferred from case law before being able to draw logical inference from it. Solving a legal problem becomes even messier when lawyers on opposing sides attribute different texts to the rules.

4   Even in parts of legal practice where the initial advice involves consideration of legal rules, the solution for the client might involve predicting what someone else will decide as well as advising what the law requires them to decide. Effectively, especially in litigious matters, lawyers might be trying to solve the same problem by several different, simultaneous routes.

5   Until recently, one of the hallmarks of most professional practice was the dominance of the professional when defining the appropriate solution. With increasing understanding of the law, rising levels of literacy, and greater access to computers, clients have an expectation that their requirements for the time, cost and manner of implementation will be taken into account in the professional definition of a successful solution.

A model should focus the thinker's mind on the process of obtaining feedback from clients at appropriate points and perhaps remind the lawyer of past conduct of lawyers found to be unacceptable by their clients, even if not unprofessional or negligent by the profession.

6   Risk taking and learning from mistakes feature particularly in creative approaches to problem solving. In acknowledging that young lawyers should be encouraged to take risks and to learn from their mistakes, the model needs to acknowledge that risks and problems which amount to professional negligence must be avoided if possible.

A model for legal problem solving should take all these factors into account. It should enable the young lawyer to continue to learn on the job. Its focus should specifically include areas in which lawyers have been found to be weak. It should remind the lawyer of the range of thinking skills – analytical, conceptual and creative – the range of actions – advise, negotiate, advocate, mediate – and the personal, organisational and professional constraints which apply to lawyers' problem solving.

A useful working model should be capable of representation in summary at a high level of generality on one page, have no more than seven features at any level of generality, and should incorporate by reference more detail which the practitioner can specifically refer to as needed.

4.6   A provisional model

The next four chapters of this book build up a provisional working model for legal problem solving in four phases:

1. Situation appraisal;
2. problem analysis;
3. Solution analysis;
4. Implementation analysis.

I have adapted the Phased Model as a starting point, because this is an approach that most readers will find familiar and hence facilitates integration of prior learning.

The first phase is Situation Appraisal discussed in Chapter 5.

4.7 Answers to Figures 4.2a-f

4.2a	Legal personality
4.2b	Executed under seal
4.2c	Action on the case
4.2d	Sine die
4.2e	Metes and bounds
4.2f	Company in General Meeting

4.8 End of chapter references and additional reading

ABA
(1991)

ABA Task Force on Law Schools and the Profession: Narrowing the Gap Tentative Draft: *Statement of Fundamental Lawyering Skills and Values*, Robert McCrate, Chair

ABA
(1992)

ABA Task Force on Law Schools and the Profession – *Final Report* ('The McCrate Report')

Amsterdam
Anthony G
(1984)

Clinical Legal Education – A 21st Century Perspective
(1984) 34 Journal of Legal Education 612

Blockley
(1992)

Engineering from Reflective Practice
(1992) 4 Research in Engineering Design 13

Coon, Dennis
(1991)

Essentials of Psychology – Exploration and Application
West Publishing Company, USA

de Bono, Edward (1992)	*Six Action Shoes* Fontana
de Bono, Edward (1985)	*Six Thinking Hats* Penguin
Gee and Jackson (1977)	*Bridging the Gap – Legal Education and Lawyer Competency* (1977) Brigham Young University Law Review 695 quoted from Cort and Sammons 29 Cle St L Review 397
Jackling, Lewis, Brandt and Sell (1990)	*Problem Solving in the Professions* Higher Education Research and Development
Kolb, David A and others (1984)	*Organisational Psychology* Prentice Hall Inc
Nathanson, Stephen (1989)	*Problem Solving in Professional Legal Education* Journal of Professional Legal Education 121
Schon, Donald (1990)	*Educating the Reflective Practitioner* Basic Books
Twining, William Miers, David (1991)	*How to do Things with Rules* (3rd ed) Law in Context Weidenfeld Paperbacks
Wallas, Graham (1926)	*The Art of Thought* Harcourt, Brace Jovanovich, Inc quoted in Albert Rothenberg and Carl R Hausmann (ed) *The Creativity Question* (1976) Duke University Press

CHAPTER

5 Situation Appraisal

> Q. An elephant, a cheetah, a rhinoceros, two chimpanzees and an anaconda all shelter under the same umbrella. How many get wet?
>
> A. None, it wasn't raining.

Anonymous joke

The Lawyer as Leader

5.1 Situation appraisal or finding the first step

Jokes often work like this. They lead your concentration up one path and away from the answer. The humour lies in discovering that you have overlooked the obvious.

Clients or other lawyers sometimes do the same thing unwittingly. Often another lawyer or a client will label a problem as *contract* or *tort* or *tax*. A young lawyer might gratefully accept the label if the client or other lawyer seems to know. It can be distressing to apply that label only to find that you are wrong and that neither the client nor the colleague is very sympathetic.

Clients want you to be their lawyer. Even lawyer colleagues want you to be their lawyer. You need to be like the cat who sniffs the air before taking another step. The more complex or unfamiliar the problem, the more you need to view it from all angles so that when you choose a path it leads you to the solution, not away from it.

5.1.1   Situation appraisal: four issues

The situation is comprised of all the institutions, people, standpoints, facts, law and possible actions that might be relevant to solving the problem. The situation is the mess from which you have to select a problem. The process of selecting the problem is the analysis. Remember that a problem for this purpose is both a situation to be resolved from the past in the form of dispute resolution (mostly referred to here as *litigation*) or as prospective action advised to be taken for the future (mostly referred to here as *commercial*).

Case 5(A)

The managing director of a client company of the firm rings for an immediate appointment with your supervisor, who is unfortunately at court. The company makes women's apparel. Another senior lawyer asks you to see the client so that some preliminary statement can be taken. The client knows that she is going to see you. When you meet her in the foyer, she thrusts five wrapped T-shirts under your nose and says:

> 'Isn't this the most disgraceful example of passing off you have ever seen? They've used our new colour range including moonlight green and passion purple. I want an injunction and I want it now.'

You are familiar with the client's product and its packaging (you buy them, wear them and like them). The test of passing off in law boils down to whether a buyer would be confused by the rival product into thinking that the maker was your client. Selecting similar colour shades and materials alone does not usually create such confusion. You sense that the client would not accept this advice from you. How do you deal with the interview so that you have time to appraise the situation properly, but make it clear that your firm will strongly advocate for the client's rights at the same time?

This type situation is not uncommon for the young lawyer. It is not just a question of applying the law to the facts, applying the facts to the law and drawing a conclusion. In addition, there are awkward threshold questions such as 'Should I be the one telling the client this?' The legal issues become not questions of knowing the text, but of making a judgment within a context and a market. 'Do I have sufficient experience of this kind of action to be making the recommendation?' The client has posed the law question as an action in passing off and put the action question squarely; 'I want an injunction, and I want it now.'

In every legal problem there will be threshold questions about who should be giving legal advice and under what circumstances. There will be law questions dealing with characterising the facts, searching for law, applying the law and predicting outcomes. There will also be action questions about what the client could do, and decisions balancing likely result time and cost, about what the client should do. The threshold questions will condition whether you can go on to consider the law questions. The law questions will largely condition the choices for the client in the action questions; but other actions might also be possible as solutions, and decision factors other than the law affect the choice. At each stage in problem solving, therefore, you will be making some contribution to answering these questions and giving advice.

We can define the content of legal problem solving as dealing with:

- Threshold issues
- Fact issues
- Law issues
- Action issues

You will know that you have completed the situation appraisal phase of problem solving when you can hypothesise about these four issues.

Threshold issues

Is there any factor constraining my acting for this client?

How might this client prefer that I communicate?

Fact issues

What is the client's version of the facts?

What independent sources for information and corroboration might be available?

Law issues

What legal topics should I be thinking about?

Action issues

What does the client want achieved?

What might be achieved within constraints of time and cost balanced against success (if litigation) or what is sought to be achieved (if commercial)?

5.1.2   The lawyer as leader

Kolb suggests that the role of the problem-solver in this phase is that of *leader*. This role is hard for the young lawyer meeting a problem or prospect for the first time, especially if the client puts the question in terms of action issues. As leader in solving the problem, the lawyer will need to:

- identify the goals and values of all the parties;
- use an expansionary mindset involving active listening, expert knowledge and previous experience, to enquire about aims and facts;
- use a contractionary mindset to classify the legal problem or prospect, to rank and prioritise possible legal questions and to identify non-legal dimensions;
- gain agreement from the client about how the problem or prospect is to be tackled that satisfies the client's aims and objectives, especially in relation to cost and time;
- act with insight into his or her own limitations as a lawyer;
- act with insight about constraints imposed in his or her own role as employee within a company, firm and within the legal profession.

In a simple problem, resolving these questions might take no more than a few minutes. In a complex problem, this might take a number of meetings, followed up with research, interspersed over a number of days or even weeks. Whether it takes minutes or days, getting the matter on the right track is the first and most important phase of problem solving.

5.1.3   Hats and shoes

In terms of De Bono hats and shoes, the leadership role suggests a number of modes. It involves white hat thinking for facts and figures and red hat thinking for emotions, intuitions and feelings. You will certainly try on the grey sneakers for investigation of facts for a time, and you might need the pink slippers for caring (see para 4.2.3 above).

5.2   Threshold issues in situation appraisal: identifying the climate

Threshold issues raise a variety of questions. The needs of the profession and the courts, the special features of the retainer between you and the client in which you are a fiduciary as well as a hired gun, the need for you to assess whether you are qualified to solve the client's problem, the rights of the client to expect that you will lead the process to a satisfactory outcome, are all factors in the contract between lawyer and client which are always present. The client will not be aware of all or of any of these issues, but the lawyer is surrounded by them. That is why I call this *the climate*.

5.2.1   A profession, not a job

Case 5(B)

> You are contacted early in the morning by a client for whom you have acted many times. She was facing criminal charges to be heard at the local magistrates' court that morning. She is sorry that she hasn't given you more notice, but she would like you to appear on her behalf to deliver a plea in mitigation, since she intends to plead guilty. She tells you that she gave the police a false name and identity. She was frightened that because of her many prior convictions she would be sent to jail. You advise her to reveal her true identity before the case is called over, because the fingerprint evidence will enable the police to establish this anyway. She does not wish to reveal her true identity. To your surprise, the police do not seem to have established her false identity. Can you speak in mitigation if you do not refer to her assumed name or refer to her character?

A solicitor was recently fined £2,000 by the Solicitors' Disciplinary Tribunal and sentenced to nine months' imprisonment suspended for two years by the Crown Court for doing something very similar to this. There is a fine line between a duty not to deceive the court and the right of the defence to put the prosecution to proof. The solicitor in this case did not have a lot of time to assess on which side of the line he stood (The Law Society (1990)).

The rules of professional conduct for solicitors and barristers sometimes mean that you cannot act for a client at all; where, for example, there is potential conflict between the new client and an existing client for whom you already act, or where the client might arguably have a suit against you for legal work done in the past.

The rules of professional conduct sometimes constrain how you must act. For example, you are not permitted to stand bail for a client even if they are a close relation, or you may not counsel your client to destroy documents which would defeat his or her case upon discovery.

Where these rules mean that a client cannot have his or her lawyer of choice, the client often regards them as bothersome and a sort of 19th century irrelevance thrown into their path.

Sometimes the rules benefit the client, as in the case of the client privilege in relation to expert opinion given in the light of pending litigation.

Your first obligation before accepting any retainer is to analyse if you (or, as an employee, your firm) are permitted to act. Most larger law firms will search their archives for conflicts by computer at the time of allocating a number to the new file. They also have elaborate procedures for checking conflicts at this time in situations where the computer search is incomplete. Smaller firms often rely upon personal knowledge of clients and their matters with the firm. This information may not be volunteered, but if you are going to be opening files yourself, you will need to ask.

Professional issues might also arise in the course of a transaction. For example, if a client ceases paying the firm in accordance with its retainer, will you be permitted to withdraw from the transaction and exercise your lien on documents? In practice, the courts are increasingly loath to leave a non-paying client without legal representation in the course of a trial but the solicitor's primary liability for counsel fees makes prepayment before trial of some practical importance.

5.2.2   Your employer

Case 5(C)

You have just started work as an assistant solicitor with a large firm in the Midlands. You work in the business law group and don't know much about the firm's practice in litigation. While taking instructions for a share purchase agreement in the absence of your supervising partner who is away on leave, the client mentions that his mother entered into a guarantee to help out his brother. His brother is now bankrupt and the bank is seeking to enforce the guarantee. The client was wondering if you could look at the question of whether the guarantee is enforceable. He thinks that the bank manager, a good friend of the brother, probably did not make it clear that the bank would actually enforce the document.

You agree to see the mother the next day and subsequently advise her that you think that she has a good case. You then get a phone call from a banking partner who is livid that you gave such advice. The firm acts for the bank in commercial transactions. While there is no conflict of interest in this case, the firm has agreed never to act against the bank in any transaction.

Even in the absence of formal conflicts or formal specialist qualifications, firms sometimes decide to restrict their practices. This is partly to do with expertise, and partly to do with cost. Large city law firms with high overheads may not feel that the fees they would need to charge for private client work such as wills, or family settlements, are fair. They establish private client departments with lower overheads or refer such work out to a firm with equal reputation and skill but a lower cost structure. Some firms feel that a commercial practice does not sit easily with a criminal or divorce practice. Not all firms will give staff written instructions about clients from whom a retainer is not to be accepted. If your firm fails to tell you, ask.

Likewise, for lawyers working in the public sector there will be agreements between authorities as to who is the appropriate body to accept instructions in cases crossing boundaries.

5.2.3 Your client or instructor

Case 5(D)

> Your firm has always acted for Paul Cossner. He is the major shareholder in a number of client companies. At first it was his name which used to be placed on files as the client. Increasingly, files have been opened in the name of the companies. Most of the companies have very little paid up capital and may not be able to pay your legal bills if they were liquidated. Your firm has been burned several times during the last recession with long standing clients going into liquidation and leaving legal fees outstanding. Recommend a policy for the firm.

In such circumstances many firms will seek a personal guarantee for fees from the directors of the company.

Of course, establishing who will be liable for legal fees is not the only reason why you need to know on whose instructions you act. It can be perilous for the lawyer to assume that one spouse may give instructions that bind the other. When a long-standing client company is placed in liquidation, the company gives instructions through the liquidator, not the majority shareholder. It is likely that the liquidator always instructs the same law firm. A company whose business has been seized by a receiver and manager gives instructions through the receiver and manager. It is likely that the receiver and manager is an accountant or other professional who always instructs the same law firm. A law firm that negotiates an employment agreement between an employee of the client company and the client company, might be seen by the employee as perfectly amicable and in no way as an adversary. The firm acts, however, only for the client company and should try to make that clear to the employee.

The information contained in Chapter 3 on personality preferences will be relevant here. Your client might be an attention-to-detail-worry-wart, or a brave free-thinking poor-grasp-on-the-details entrepreneur. One of your roles in situation appraisal is to assess the strengths and likely failings of the client as a partner in solving their own problem. Clients who are weak on detail might need more reminders and more in writing. Clients who lose sight of the big picture might need occasional counselling about issues worth fighting for, and those worth settling.

Certain transactions seem to invite certain personality issues. Characteristically, clients buying a small business such as a take away food franchise are glowingly optimistic about the likely success of the venture. They often commit themselves prior to establishing the financial viability of the venture, and see your role as magically 'putting it in writing' rather than helping them negotiate the terms of the purchase. Another example might be a couple who are complaining about the terrible job the builder did on their house renovations. They will be as passionately involved in the suit as they would if they were involved in a divorce.

It is not your role to change you client's personality, but your leadership can sometimes only be exercised by anticipating the client's behaviour.

5.2.4   You

Case 5(E)

You work in a small practice in the north. One of the things that you like about this practice is that you have seen clients yourself from your first day of employment. You have developed a bit of a speciality in copyright law for authors. On the recommendation of another client, you see a couple who were commissioned as consultants to prepare a report for an association of independent book sellers about staff pilfering of goods.

The consultants want to publish some of the figures at an international conference in support of this problem. They will not identify the source of the figures. This is a big opportunity for them to establish themselves as leaders in the field. The book association is adamant that they may not do this. There was never any discussion between the association and the consultants about copyright issues. The older consultant is a gentleman with white hair and a short temper. He makes it clear that he thinks you are too young and inexperienced to give him advice, although he is happier to be paying your hourly rate than the rate of a partner.

It is rare for clients to assault the competence of the lawyer directly, although many are concerned to be dealing with practitioners much younger than them. No lawyer would ever develop skills if he or she refused to accept unfamiliar matters. On the other hand, matters entirely beyond present experience should involve a more experienced practitioner, either as counsel or supervisor. Clients who do not voice overt concerns but who are quietly concerned will often be assuaged by a purposeful, calm approach. It is best for the lawyer to openly acknowledge that both research and consultation with senior colleagues will take place before final advice is rendered. The client will usually approve of such an approach. Clients who voice overt concerns might sometimes be prepared to pay for a more senior lawyer to deal with the matter direct.

There is no magic formula to establishing credibility but the following tips may be useful:

- act early, not late;
- act first on the things that worry the client as well as taking steps on the matters that worry you;
- show interest and listen well;
- research the client's relationship with the firm;

- discuss the matter with other lawyers so that you can quote those discussions;
- above all, never be defensive about age or inexperience.

(See Chapman *Interviewing and Counselling*.)

On a rare occasion, the sanest thing for you to do will be to retire gracefully from the fray!

5.3   The fact and law issues in situation appraisal

5.3.1   Calibrating the problem and its dimensions

Case 5(F) 'A roof over their heads'

Your clients are Mr and Mrs Xenos. They run a business as roofing contractors in the outer suburbs of a large city. They borrowed money secured by collateral mortgages on some jointly owned property. They have a 50 page, professionally drawn, loan agreement. They hand this document over to you at the interview. They have fallen into arrears in repayment. Although they have tried to negotiate for more time, they have been sued on the loan agreement. The terms of settlement for this suit effectively reduced the interest rate and extended the time for payment of the arrears and principal. They also give you copies of the settlement agreement.

They are not dissatisfied with the work of their former solicitor. They were just told by a friend that you are a terrific negotiator and might be able to get them even more favourable terms for repayment. They are concerned that they may still have to sell their home to make the repayments. They feel that the economy will pick up and that they will be able to repay the principal sum by selling a property, but would prefer to ensure that the timing is right.

What would you do at the first interview?

This story is based on a real client file that I have modified and adapted for use as a role play in client interviewing. Most young lawyers acting this problem as a role play spend most of their interview time assiduously reading the loan agreement and the terms of settlement, even though clients have further facts to give about the background to the debt if they are asked.

In reality, it is unlikely that a professionally drawn, lengthy loan agreement will be defective or afford the borrower any relief. A better solution for the client is more likely to be found in the circumstances surrounding the loan or its execution, not in the document itself. Presumably the lawyers who acted for Mr and Mrs Xenos in the settlement of the law suit limited their instructions to this story, too.

Case 5(G) 'A roof over their heads' – further facts

Mr and Mrs Xenos have run a successful roofing business for the last 20 years. They are conservative people. Until five years ago they had used very few tax saving measures. Five years ago, their brother-in-law found a new accountant. He suggested that they gain some tax relief by investing in a scheme to breed stud racing horses. Most of the money to be invested was borrowed from the bank and the interest payments to service the borrowings were tax deductible, hence the tax savings. The scheme was promoted by a public company in which the accountant had a financial interest, although this was not disclosed until much later. (Although the accountant told them this was a scheme only on offer to his own clients, they know at least one friend of a client who rang and enquired about investing in it. The friend took up units but later sold his interest to a third party.)

Three years ago, during a recession in the building industry, the revenue from the roofing business dropped by three quarters. For a time, though, interest rates kept on increasing. Even though their income was reduced, Mr and Mrs Xenos still had to make the interest payments. They fell behind. The promoter of the investment scheme offered to lend them the interest payments in arrears and the principal, in effect reorganising the loan. Mr and Mrs Xenos accepted that they had just been caught with the times and were grateful for this offer, particularly since the interest rate offered by the promoter in the new arrangement was lower than that their bank (the original lender) was currently offering. They signed the formal loan agreement then.

The inevitable happened. Shortly after this, Mr and Mrs Xenos fell behind in their payments again, resulting in the compromised suit they told you about. The only way they could pay this debt would be to sell their own house and a small cottage in the country. They fear being left destitute.

The further facts reveal additional potential sources of relief-conflict of interest on the part of the accountant and a possibility that the scheme entered into was one that required the issue of a prospectus. The second line of enquiry might provide an entire defence to payment under the loan, and indeed entitle Mr and Mrs Xenos to the return of all the money paid under the scheme.

Both these lines of enquiry are being pursued in the real case from which these facts were taken.

5.3.2 Finding the right words for the law and the fact issues

When Mr and Mrs Xenos come to you, they come to you with a highly concrete picture of their problem. They are concerned that they may have to sell their home (see figure 5.1).

Figure 5.1

Your picture is different. You need to find which book to take off the shelf (see figure 5.2).

Figure 5.2

At law school, often the toughest issue has been solved by the curriculum. When you are given a snail in a bottle problem in subject called *Torts*, you know that the problem can be characterised as dealing with the law of tort. When a client comes to you, however, with a pirate recording, or a plagiarised novel, you have to find the label. Is it *copyright, confidential information* or *passing off,* or a combination of some or all?

This process of labelling is about language and is often highly abstract. We have to translate the clients concrete facts into our abstract language. The snail in the bottle causing pain and suffering becomes manufacturer's breach of duty, and the client's objective of compensation, quickly translates as damages claimed through a litigious transaction.

The situation appraisal stage involves working through the law issues that need to be resolved to meet the client's objectives. In the case of *A roof over their heads*, we have already seen that several legal issues are a possibility:

- the validity of the original scheme (company law);
- the actions of accountant in the original advice (negligence);
- actions of the accountant when the clients entered in the loan agreement (breach of fiduciary duty).

In summary, the first step in formulating the law issues is to find a match between concrete client words and abstract law words.

5.4   Thinking through the legal issues

When first given a legal problem to deal with, everyone doodles. You will list, cull, select, prioritise and sequence items on the list. The doodles often give you a trail to follow about how you deal with the issues of Threshold, Law, Fact and Action.

You will add to the things to think about when they strike you as relevant. Items added could be facts: from the client, the climate, corroborating or contradicting sources. They could be the expectations: of you, your firm, the other side or their client, or of cost and time. They could be issues of substantive or procedural law: a rule, a principle, an exception.

When you add something to the list in situation appraisal you will be using an expansionary thinking mode. Mostly you will use them tacitly. When you run out of items to add to the list, it is useful to practise consciously a few other thinking tools as a check to see that you have added all that might be helpful.

The following tools in expansionary mode are discussed below for this stage:

- active listening;
- constructing the issues for the other side;
- brainstorming;
- preparing a mind map;
- doing a problem solving walkaround;
- looking wider.

At some point in situation appraisal, you start dismissing items as being irrelevant or of no use. Examples might be facts from the client's business that are not relevant to the issue but were given great importance by the client and a client statement based on opinion that can only be proved by expert evidence. The client's expectation that the whole matter will be resolved in a week might be struck from the list. You might have decided that the loan agreement in itself is valid and enforceable and so have struck the possibility of seeking to re-open that judgment from your list.

Every time you delete something from your list of items to think about, you are using contractionary forms of thinking. You mostly used these forms of thinking tacitly, but when you think that you have completed the task, it is useful to try another few modes consciously, as a check.

The following thinking tools for thinking in contractionary mode are dealt with in this chapter:

- a threshold check for change;
- checking client expectations and resources;
- comparison to similar fact situations;
- placing the hypothesis in question form.

5.4.1 A checklist

The processes of thinking in expansionary and contractionary
mode, together with some of the topics thought about during
situation appraisal are summarised in a checklist at figure 5.3. It is
a checklist because it will allow you to hover over the topics,
thinking about them in no particular order and ordering them in
the sequence most productive for you and your problem.

SITUATION APPRAISAL

> **AND YOU**

11. CONTRACT THE LIST BY DELETING IRRELEVANT ITEMS AND BY IDENTIFYING RELATIONSHIPS BETWEEN IDEAS

BECAUSE OF

12. FACTS RELEVANT TO THE HYPOTHESIS NOTING

13. Changes in:
- ☐ the climate,
- ☐ gaps,
- ☐ omissions,
- ☐ inconsistencies,
- ☐ facts requiring corroboration,
- ☐ impact of the rules of evidence

14. YOUR CALIBRATION OF THE PROBLEM

15. Is the problem:
- ☐ Big/small,
- ☐ long/short,
- ☐ hard/easy,
- ☐ standard/special,
- ☐ general/specialist

16. YOUR ASSESSMENT OF THE CLIMATE

17. EXCLUDING PROBLEMS THAT:
- ☐ not your problem,
- ☐ not the firm's problem,
- ☐ not a problem for the legal profession

18. YOUR ASSESSMENT OF THE CLIENT'S EXPECTATIONS

19. Counselling the client to amend goals where necessary

20. TO LIST:

21. Law issues for research and facts for follow-up

22. Possible solutions on the action list

23. FOR CONSIDERATION IN MORE DETAIL AT THE PROBLEM ANALYSIS PHASE

 **CONTRACTIONARY MODE**

Figure 5.3

> **WHEN YOU ANALYSE A CLIENT'S PROPOSAL OR STORY YOU:**

1. EXPAND THE LIST OF ITEMS TO CONSIDER

BY

2. LISTENING ANALYTICALLY & INTUITIVELY NOTING

3. FACTS in client's story or proposal OBJECTIVES AND EXPECTATIONS

4. THE CLIMATE,
☐ the Client,
☐ you,
☐ the Firm,
☐ the other side

5. THINKING CREATIVELY BY

6. ☐ brainstorming,
☐ looking wider,
☐ arguing for the other side,
☐ creating a mind map

7. MATCHING LANGUAGE FROM

8. The client's story or proposal

with

9. Relevant legal concepts

10. FORMING A HYPOTHESIS ABOUT THE CLIENT'S PROBLEMS OR PROPOSAL THAT EXPRESS LAW IN THE FORM OF QUESTIONS

◀||||||▶ **EXPANSIONARY MODE**

© Margot Costanzo 1994

5.5   Tools for expansionary thinking in situation appraisal

5.5.1   Active listening

Practitioners are often so conscious of the information they need to gather in order to start solving a problem that they forget to give the client an opportunity to develop an overview of his or her needs or concerns before moving into the detail. The person who listens is the person who is able to assess the credibility, intelligence and needs of the speaker. It is surprising how much of this information can be gleaned by having the client speak for five minutes when you first meet. Lawyers often avoid this because they claim that clients waste their time and ramble. If your purpose is to assess credibility, intelligence and needs, *what* the client says is often less important than *how* it is said and *why* items are included or omitted. One learns new information by active listening (see *Interviewing and Counselling* by Jenny Chapman in this series para 4.2 and *Negotiation* by Diana Tribe para 2.1.1).

5.5.2   Construct the case for the other side

In a litigious matter, it is helpful to test the weakness in your own client's case by postulating the story from the perspective of other people involved, particularly that of the adversary. This might reveal weakness in your client's version of the facts, in the credibility of the client and others as witnesses or in arguments of law. The client may not be much interested in arguments from the other side. In many commercial situations, parties with separate legal representation assume that they are adversaries. Their instructions to their lawyer, therefore, are likely to focus on avenues of difference. It is always helpful to list what people have in common and to look at their underlying interests in a transaction. (See *Negotiation* by Diana Tribe in this series at para 1.3.3.)

5.5.3   Brainstorm

This can be done both with the client and with other lawyers. The essence of brainstorming is to separate the listing process from the evaluation process. Culling the list too early can be fatal to finding a good solution. Perhaps when we do this we are thinking of the aphorism that the shortest distance between two points is a straight line. We think that if we find a starting point quickly we shall be able to follow it to its conclusion. Readers who live in large cities might have already modified this aphorism by preferring the longer route with less traffic. Even in journeys, shorter is not always quicker.

Movement in the mind is not about distance but about time. The quickest way of solving a problem is rarely a straight line. At best a spiral, the route of the mind is mostly a doodled mess. When we first starting thinking about a problem, we have a jumble of observations and thoughts. When reading through 'A roof over their heads' (para 5.3.1) you might have jotted down the following:

* roofing business

* 20 years

* loan

* arrears

* very honest clients

* want time to pay

* tax advice

You can brainstorm at any phase in the problem solving process. You can brainstorm alone or with others. Assuming that there are no constraints on your acting (Threshold issues, see para 5.2 above) you can go on to ask some questions relating to the Fact, Law and Action issues. In brainstorming about the Action issue, always imagine an outcome that would exceed the expectations that the client has explained, as well as one that is less. Try to be fanciful. Do not censor the list. Ninety seconds of uninterrupted brainstorming will give you a lot of material.

You can obtain ideas for the Fact, Law and Action issues by taking any word at random from a dictionary and asking what that word suggests about the situation. The same can be done for any image from a magazine. If the word or image suggests nothing abandon it and find another. You might find that you can obtain lots of fertile ideas by just thinking about your other files.

From time to time review the list, cull items that are not relevant. Start again if you feel you have not seen enough of the situation.

5.5.4   Mind maps

Chapter 2 (at para 2.3) showed how all problem solvers can be seduced into forming a premature view of the problem and its solution because our perception of the problem becomes fixed very quickly.

You can perceive the problem from different perspectives by making a mind map of the notes you have taken (Buzan 1977).

A mind map is a non-linear means of representing the relationships between ideas incorporating colour, symbols and key words. Two mind maps prepared by two different lawyers setting out the associations that the word 'contract' brought to mind for them are set out in figure 5.4 (see also *Advocacy* by Andy Boon in this series at para 1.3). They omit images and are not printed in colour. They are, therefore, modified mind maps.

Figure 5.4 (1)

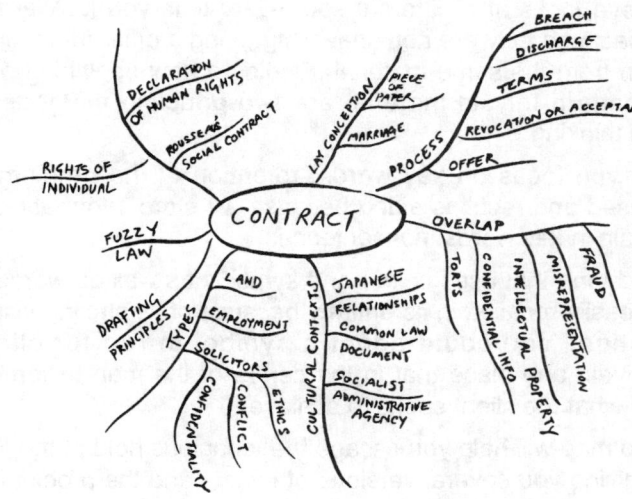

Figure 5.4 (2)

Mind maps have a number of advantages:

- Your eye looks at a different spot every time you look at the map because they are non-linear, triggering a different thought pattern from the same material. Finding a new beginning or a new pattern for old material are two principle methods of lateral thinking.

- When you focus on key words, retention of the problem is increased and recall is aided because we store information in the brain in key words, not sentences.

- A mind map that uses colour and symbols as well as words is more easily recalled in its entirety because of its striking visual depiction. You could adopt a symbol in red for client objectives, and place that in the centre of the map to remind you of what the client seeks to achieve.

A mind map will help you escape the tenacious hold of the first view, by giving you several versions of events and the problem at your first sitting.

5.5.5   Problem walkaround

Ned Herrmann (Herrmann 1989) suggests that all problems should be viewed from four perspectives:

- A rational analytical perspective: what do we know?

- An organisational perspective: what might we do?

- The perspective of how the situation might affect other people: how will other people behave/react?

- A holistic, conceptual future oriented perspective: how else might the problem be described?

5.5.6   Look wider

In the case of 'A roof over their heads', a more fruitful solution was found by looking at the surrounding circumstances of the loan and by delving further into the history of the transaction. Looking more widely might involve looking at the story in more detail, hearing it from more people, looking further back in time, coming closer to the present, looking into the future. Certainly at first one calibrates the dimensions of the problem instinctively. When you begin a new problem, look wide rather than narrow.

5.6   Tools for contractionary thinking in situation appraisal

Contractionary thinking will cause you to delete some items from your list and to start to pattern the others by the relationships that connect ideas. At the end of the situation appraisal phase, you should be aiming to have formed a hypothesis about the problem, preferably in question form, and to have identified what further facts are needed. You will then be ready for the next phase.

5.6.1   Threshold issue

At the situation appraisal stage, you should be certain that you can answer the following questions:

- May your organisation act at all?
- Should you act? Subject to supervision, alone?
- Which parts of the client's story are another person's problem? (ie more appropriately dealt with by an accountant, psychologist etc.)
- Are there difficult personality issues for you, the client, the other side, the other side's lawyer?
- Are there other professional issues which suggest constraints on how you act or what you do?

In the case of 'A roof over their heads', there are no facts that suggest that the particular lawyer should not act. It is likely to be a complex matter that will require expert legal advice and the tactical expertise of a good litigator and some parts of the litigation might require a financial expert.

One example of a personality issue is that clients who are honest can be open to manipulation by unscrupulous parties.

They might believe that they have incurred a financial obligation, the issue is whether it can be enforced.

5.6.2 Client objectives and expectations

Client objectives will often be comparable to the straits of Gibraltar through which you are required to navigate. Establishing realistic client objectives and expectations are often a separate negotiation. The client will only give you instructions that satisfy his or her objectives and expectations. The client will often come with these pre-conceived, or misconceived. You might need to explain some issues in law so that the client's expectations and objectives are realistic.

5.6.3 Comparison to similar situations

The experienced practitioner will have a storehouse of other similar cases from which to form analogies potentially relevant to the problem under examination. Experience enables the practitioner to say whether the instant case is exceptional or normal, whether it will be simple or complex, whether most of the work will be in the diagnosis or in the implementation.

A practitioner dealing a problem for the first time should arm him or herself with half a dozen similar situations and their outcomes. One will not be enough to give a picture of the range of possible considerations and events. Reported cases are not as good as actual files because reports contain only issues and activities relevant to the judgment. Procedural, tactical, cost, time, client and firm issues will be revealed from actual files.

5.6.4 A working hypothesis in question form

It is helpful to resist defining the problem. First set out the problem as a hypothesis. A hypothesis is a theory about the problem and how it might be solved. We know that hypotheses need to be verified. We know that in formulating a hypothesis we need to look for invalid assumptions, and also at the things that are not there (which Sherlock Holmes thought so important; see para 2.3.4).

In the case of 'A roof over their heads', the clients defined their problem as how to get more time to pay. We have discovered that this problem definition assumes that they are obliged to pay. If we form a hypothesis about each of the four issues, we might have notes that look like this.

- Threshold issue

    No problems about acting.

- Fact issues

    Chronology of events?

    Copies of all documents?

    Possible witnesses?

    Corroboration of representations made by the accountant?

- Law issues

    Loan agreement defective in form?

    Undue influence surrounding the agreement?

    Professional negligence on the part of the accountant who advised the clients to enter the race-horse breeding scheme?

    Conflict of interest on the part of the accountant who advised the clients to enter into the loan agreement with the promoter of the accountant has an interest in the promoter company?

    Original scheme unenforceable because it amounted to an offer to the public that was not supported by a prospectus but was required to?

- Action issue

    A meeting with the lender/promoter/accountant to verify the facts and get their side of the story before they know that we might be seeking to re-open the whole claim.

5.7   Situation appraisal: a summary of the four issues

Once we have prepared the working hypothesis (see above), we shall have addressed most of the Threshold issues and established some lines of enquiry for the Fact and Law issues. In some situations, we might have very firm ideas about what we/the client might do in the Action issue. In the case of '*A roof over their heads*' we have a tentative initial step to meet the other parties, but a decision on what to do may first require further analysis of the Law issue. This further analysis takes place in the next phase of the problem solving process – problem analysis.

5.8   End of chapter references and additional reading

Tony Buzan   *Make the Most of Your Mind* Pan
(1977)

Ned Herrmann   *The Creative Brain* LakeLure
(1989)

The Law Society   *The Guide to the Professional Conduct of*
(1990)   *Solicitors*

CHAPTER

6 Problem Analysis

Patient: Doctor, doctor, my hair is falling out. Can you give me something to keep it in?

Doctor: Here's a paper bag.

Anonymous joke

The Lawyer as Investigator

6.1   Problem analysis: four issues

Even where both the client and the professional agree on their respective roles, the approach of the professional in defining the problem and suggesting solutions is often something of a mystery to the client.

The situation appraisal phase (Chapter 5) should have enabled you to decide that you may act and to develop some preliminary thoughts on how. It also should have established:

- the client's objectives;
- a hypothesis about how the law might solve the client's problem;
- lines of enquiry about the facts;
- lines of enquiry about law;
- some possibilities about what might be done.

In the problem analysis phase, you will be spending most of the time selecting, defining and applying concepts and drawing inferences. It is mostly a tacit thinking process. In this thinking process, you will be spending most of your time on the Fact and Law issues, although you might add a possibility or two to the list of Action issues. You will also need to pass by the Threshold issue to check for change.

In the problem analysis phase, the following questions are relevant.

Threshold issues

Has there been any change in the climate, the facts or the law since the last time this problem was looked at?

Fact issues

What are the relevant facts in this story?

Which need corroboration, addition or other investigation?

Does the law of evidence suggest any special investigations for the facts?

Law issues

How can I define the legal issues?

Applying the law to the facts, what does the law say?

Do the client's expectations or objectives need to be modified?

Action issues

What does the application of the law to both the facts and the client's objectives suggest might be done?

What does the client want done?

6.1.1   The lawyer as investigator – hat and shoes

Kolb suggests that the role of the problem solver in this phase is that of investigator. It requires blue hat thinking to design a thinking scheme for the particular problem. Certainly in all cases you will use white hat thinking to look for the facts and figures, and to hunt out the law and you will use the red hat to bring emotions, intuitions and feelings to the surface. This phase also requires that you try out the grey sneakers – snooping about to get to relevant facts, objectives and law.

If situation appraisal is like the big cat sniffing the air before choosing a path, problem appraisal is like the helicopter with a searchlight trained on the fleeing gang seeking only the ringleader.

6.1.2   The relationship of fact and law

Most of the problem analysis phase concentrates on defining and refining the Fact and Law issues. The Fact and Law issues involve a complex relationship between fact and law.

Case 6(A)

On 11 January 1990, David Burgin, a country solicitor, purchased a Christmas Bonus Instant Lottery ticket. The ticket bore the general inscription *win up to £200,000 dollars instantly!* It presented three games, each following the Christmas theme.

The first game depicted a rectangle with six Christmas trees in two columns of three trees sitting on a present box. The instructions were *scratch all 6 trees. match 3 numbers and win. scratch the present to reveal your prize up to £200,000.*

The second game depicted nine wrapped presents in three columns of three. The instructions were *scratch all gift boxes. match 3 amounts and win that prize up to £200,000 instantly!*

The third game depicted a jolly Santa. The instructions read *scratch santa and count the gifts. 2 gifts win free ticket. 3 gifts win £20. 4 gifts win £200.*

Mr Burgin played all three games. When he scratched the two columns of Christmas trees in the first game, the following numbers were revealed:

7 1

3 7

3 1

Mr Burgin contended that by matching 7/7, 3/3 and 1/1 he had 'matched three numbers' and was therefore entitled to win. The prize was £20,000.

But what was the valid definition of the legal issue? The first definition proposed required the construction of the word *match* in the first game only. One of the meanings of the word *match* and its common everyday meaning is *to pair*. On this problem definition, Mr Burgin had to win.

A second definition of the legal issue was possible. The legal issue could be defined as requiring the construction of the word *match* in both the first and the second games. If one presumed that it most likely meant the same in both games, the answer was in more doubt. The reference to *win that prize* implied that three of the same items were to be revealed, not three pairs of items. The wider problem definition would, therefore, be fatal to Mr Burgin's entitlement.

On appeal, two of the judges opted for the first and narrower definition of the problem and found for Mr Burgin who later collected the prize of £25,000. Those judges added in the alternative that there was no reason to assume that each game would have the same rules. The dissenting judge opted for the wider definition and found against Mr Burgin. The lottery authorities must have been delighted that the case was only decided three years after the original purchase. 45% of similar lottery tickets would have resulted in similar wins for the purchasers, but presumably most had been thrown away by the time the case received publicity. (*State Lotteries Office v Burgin* (1993) unreported decision of the Supreme Court of New South Wales, Court of Appeal.)

This simple case nicely illustrates the circular process of problem definition in law. The question of which facts are deemed relevant will to some extent depend upon your view of the legal issues. Likewise, characterising the relevant legal issues will also depend on how the facts actually present or are actually presented. If the games had been presented separately on three different tickets, it might have been harder to argue for the wider definition of the legal issue because the presumption of uniformity in the use of the word *match* would have been less powerful. Each game could more clearly be regarded as a separate contract.

In a litigious case, the investigation of facts in the Law issue will concentrate on finding those that are ultimately provable and admissible as evidence. The confusing and difficult aspect about the relativity of law and fact is that relevance is determined by the relationship of one to the other. When in doubt, it is always best to start with the facts.

6.2   The Fact issues

Whether something will be regarded as a fact is a complex question. Facts may be used to meet different objectives depending on whether they are sought solely in order to make out a legal issue, or to motivate an action issue.

6.2.1   Persuasive facts and evidence

Case 6(B)

> Francesca's client was a small family company that had run the local department store for the last three generations. They had branched out into property development in a small way, renovating a row of six cottages for rent. The builder had not done a good job on the finish, a miscellany of small things done poorly or not at all which added up to a significant sum if they were to be rectified. Counsel said that there was really no question of law and that they should be able to settle early in the piece. Counsel needed details about the faults in workmanship to persuade the other side to reach an early settlement.

> Although the cottages were not due for further inspections from the local authority, Francesca arranged for the building surveyor to make an exhaustive inspection of all the faults. It made quite an impressive list. The client and counsel were both appalled at what Francesca had done. She could not understand why.

Francesca's client now runs the risk that the local authority will require all kinds of rectification works to be done. The client had actually planned to make as much fuss about non-compliance as possible to achieve a good settlement before trial. He had hoped to avoid obtaining direct testimony from building inspectors at the local authority, because the defects were obvious on a site inspection.

He had wanted to use the payment in damages to reduce the mortgage, not to rectify the works. It is true that at some stage in the litigation, evidence might have been required of the nature of the deficient work either from the building surveyor or from a building expert. In the early phase, however, facts that would not formally amount to evidence might be persuasive and cheaper.

6.2.2   Admissible and inadmissible facts

Evidentiary facts need to be logically relevant to the issue, attested to by a person who holds personal expert knowledge, and not simply opinion or proven as required. In a criminal trial it is the prosecution who bears the onus of proof beyond reasonable doubt. In a civil trial, the person seeking to establish certain facts, either as claim or counterclaim or defence, bears the burden of proof on the balance of probabilities. The onus of proof and the burden of proof can have significant practical ramifications because a case known is not a case proven. To prove a case might cost a lot of money and consume lawyer and client time (see generally, *Cross on Evidence* (1986)).

6.2.3   Logically relevant or irrelevant facts

Facts can be reasons for action in the commercial situation or evidence to prove a case in the litigious situation.

As reasons for action, there is no formal test of whether an item of information is a fact. A rumour about the intentions of a competitor might be sufficient to justify your client outlaying significant sums to counter those intentions. Although a good commercial lawyer will always take the time to check that the grounds for the client's actions are logical, at the end of the day, it is the client who must be satisfied that the actions he or she intends to take are rational. In business, the test will usually be whether the actions will increase profit or reduce risk.

In the litigious situation, on the other hand, facts might begin as mere rumour but will become evidence only if they pass certain stringent legal tests. Evidence must embody information that is logically probative, derives from a competent source and must not fall within certain exclusionary rules.

The hearsay rule is the exclusionary rule that troubles non-lawyers. Hearsay is any evidence tendered to prove a fact in issue by a person who is not in court to be cross-examined about it. To anyone other than a lawyer, it can result in some strange decisions about admissibility, particularly in criminal cases. These special rules require special explanation.

The similar fact evidence exception to the hearsay rule might permit facts about previous similar criminal offences having been committed, even where the accused has not been charged or convicted of an offence in respect of them. It is said that facts indicating a psychological propensity of the client without more will not be admissible. The line between mere propensity (and therefore excluded) and more than propensity (and therefore admissible) is not clear. In the case of *Noor Mohamed v R* [1949] AC 182 the appellant had been accused of murdering his mistress with cyanide. He was a goldsmith and used cyanide in his trade. At the trial, the judge admitted evidence showing that he had previously killed a wife by tricking her into swallowing cyanide as a cure for toothache. This decision was overturned on appeal to the Privy Council.

In the civil arena, the hearsay rule would exclude evidence, in a claim for worker's compensation by the worker's wife, of statements made by her husband about the cause of injuries that led to his later death (*Amys v Barton* [1912] KB 40 (CA)). The hearsay rule would also justify the exclusion of evidence about the temperature reading on a thermometer as observed by a witness, unless elaborate evidence verifying thermometers in general, and that thermometer in particular, is tendered (*R v Pettigrew* (1980) 71 Cr App R 39 (CA)).

The hearsay rule also results in some labyrinthine arguments that seem unnecessary even to other lawyers. In the case of *R v Rice and others* [1963] 1 QB 857, an airline ticket was admitted as original evidence even though no witnesses were called to verify its issue and in normal circumstances would have been excluded under the hearsay rule unless so verified.

The appeal judgment does not explain clearly for what purpose the airline ticket was being admitted if not to prove that the persons named on the ticket travelled to the destination on the date given (Cross (1969) 7 MULR 1). Now a lawyer seeking to adduce an airline ticket into evidence as part of the proof that the person named on it travelled to the named destination on that date will be required to have regard to these complex provisions.

Occasionally, even the judges are prepared to make exceptions to the hearsay rule based on the sorts of considerations that lay persons would use. For example, when Lord St Leonards died many years after retiring as Lord Chancellor, and his will could not be found, evidence of the content of the will discussed with many of his colleagues during his lifetime was admitted as an exception to the hearsay rule because the probability of it being valid proof of the contents of the will was thought to be high (*Sugden v Lord St Leonards* (1876) 1 PD 154). (The will was described in the report as 'being of great length and complexity'. The picture of Lord Chancellor's colleagues setting up lookouts in the corridor so they could scuttle away and thus avoid the umpteenth conversation on the contents of his will is irresistible!)

Statutory exceptions to the hearsay rule sometimes result in cumbersome procedures. In some jurisdictions, microfiche of accounting records can be verified by statutory declaration or affidavit of the person who made the microfiche to the effect that the microfiche is a complete record etc. Often a statutory declaration is prepared at the time the microfiche are made and that, too is placed on microfiche (against the possibility that the person making the microfiche may not be available when the verification is required.) One might ask whether the statutory declaration on microfiche itself requires verification?

These considerations are set out to remind you that there is a gap between the lawyer's version of facts in use and how they might be proved, and the facts in the clients' mind. You might need to spend considerable time explaining that gap as part of educating your client's expectations about a viable decision on the Action issues.

Of course, these considerations do not trouble all contentious disputes. There are an ever growing number of administrative tribunals not bound by the rules of evidence deciding important questions.

6.2.4   Facts and opinion

A patient may testify about how he or she felt and the symptoms of illness. Only an expert, such as a physician, may give admissible evidence about the medical cause of the patient's symptoms. The patient's evidence is regarded as evidence of facts of which the patient has personal knowledge. The doctor's evidence is regarded as an opinion requiring inferences to be drawn about the facts, the capacity to draw those inferences requiring special knowledge.

Other categories of conclusions are required to be attested to by experts. A layperson can testify as to the identity of handwriting, the weather, the state of the roads, the state of someone's health, a state of intoxication, whether a voice was male or female and whether a publication has a tendency to deprave or corrupt. However, as lawyers recognise the expertise of other callings, more and more items have been added to the list of evidence requiring an expert.

Opinion evidence is rarely presented neutrally for the guidance of the court. It is most often part of each party's argument so that the court is in the position of having to choose between experts when there is conflict. The credibility of the expert, as proven by qualification and experience and the demeanour of the expert in the box will more often win the day than the inherent logic of the opinion being expressed. Court proceedings about compensation for physical injury or defective building often amount to a question of whose expert is preferred by the jury (where they are the trier of fact) or the judge (if it is not a jury trial). Increasingly, court rules are abandoning the concept of trial by ambush – where you arrive at court not really knowing what the other expert is going to say – and moving to a full disclosure of expert opinion before the trial. It is hoped that the requirement for disclosure will facilitate preparation for the trial.

Scientists are particularly critical of the use of expert scientific opinion such as forensic evidence in a trial. Scientific proof sets out to eliminate possible causes based on statistical probability; legal proof, on the other hand, sets out to prove likely causes based on tests of probability; tests such as *beyond reasonable doubt* or *more likely than not* (Bourke (1993)).

6.2.5   Fact and future transactions

If the problem to be solved involves agreements about future rights and obligations between the parties, the rules of evidence will not naturally apply. This does not mean that a lawyer need not require proof. Clients will understandably make assumptions about ownership of assets, use of business names or tenure of leases. The lawyer must always seek corroboration. The lawyer will, therefore, search the company records to verify its registered name and shareholding; call for a copy of a written assignment of copyright or chose in action because they are only validly assigned if in writing; search a title; and obtain certificates from authorities who can levy taxes and impose charges on land.

All authorities charge for searches and certificates. Clients frequently complain about these fees, particularly when the fees are for you to obtain a certificate of incorporation of their own company to verify the date of incorporation or company name because they cannot find the original! It is never advisable to assume that the client's perception of the facts is correct. It would not be unknown for a client to have misspelled the company name and to have misquoted the date of its incorporation for the company's entire existence!

6.3   The Law issue: the law

Law discussions by lawyers feature three themes: finding the law, understanding and analysing the law as content, and applying the law to facts. Law school focuses on the products of legal thinking, the written or oral arguments on given facts and the judgments about given problems. But those arguments are preceded by a process of thinking that happens in the mind not on the page (*Legal Research* by David Stott and *Advocacy* by Andy Boon in this series deal with these topics).

Some jurisprudential commentators, on the other hand, have tried to focus on what happens in the mind. Posner is not the only jurisprudential commentator or judge to point out that legal reasoning extends beyond techniques of scientific enquiry or formal logic (Posner (1990)). He describes some of the techniques of practical reasoning used by judges including forms of hypothesis testing, intuition (in the form of presuppositions of which we might at best be dimly aware), or 'tacit knowing'.

Sometimes it is helpful to rise above the process of tacit knowing and to formalise one's thought processes when drawing relationships between ideas. Try to imagine thinking as a journey; if you carry a map of the journey in your mind's eye, it is easier to retrace your steps back to a valid starting point if you make a mistake at one point. You can also only work in relay with another lawyer if you can describe where you've been and why (so you don't cover the same ground), and then describe where you want to meet.

6.3.1   Authority, language and logic

Reasoning through legal issues involves three formal topics. You reason about:

- authority (using the rules of precedent, hierarchy of the courts);
- language (using dictionary and common meanings and authoritative meanings from statutes or cases);

- logic (whether the statements under the inferences are correct and whether the conclusions are logically justifiable).

Each of these reasoning processes shade into one another, but they have specialised and individual processes at their core.

In Chapter 5, I described the process of thinking through the situation appraisal phase as one of adding items to a list that you sort, arrange and cull. Perhaps it is time to be a little more formal.

6.3.2 Co-ordination and subordination

When you reason in each of these ways, you follow only two processes: co-ordination and subordination (see also *Legal Writing* by Margot Costanzo in this series at para 4.2.4).

Co-ordinate

List the ideas that need to be taken into account. They are *co-ordinate* ideas when they are at the same level of generality.

Subordinate

Subordination involves classification and patterning. They will be *subordinate* ideas as soon as you structure them at different levels of generality and decide that one point must logically precede others.

When you classify, you state which ideas relate to which other ideas under the same general concept. In the case of 'A roof over their heads' (Chapter 5) you would classify the facts in accordance with their relevance to the basic topics you identified as possible hypotheses in the situation appraisal stage. So you might classify facts for their relevance in relation to the company law issues, the loan issues and the issues dealing with the negligence or breach of fiduciary duty of the accountant. You would classify thoughts about the law in the same way.

When you pattern ideas you identify relationships within each classification. Patterns used in legal problem solving are:

- logic
- time
- structure
- values

(See *Legal Writing* by Margot Costanzo in this series at para 7.3.)

In the case of 'A roof over their heads', you would use time to pattern the facts, values to establish the relative importance of the possible legal remedies, logic to relate the facts to the law and referential structure to sequence the discussion of how law ideas apply to the facts and the conclusions that might be drawn from them.

Often the ideas belonging one classification will be involved in different patterns. The fact that a loan agreement was signed by the clients will figure in a time relationship when listing the clients' instructions but will also re-appear as one of the key features in a logic pattern when applying facts to law.

Analyse some of your own written arguments. You might find that you make some slips common to lawyers. Do you use the language of logical inference (*therefore, however,* or *accordingly*), implying *subordination*, when you only mean to add another idea to the list ie *co-ordination*? Do you list law ideas but forget to sequence them so that the reader knows their relative importance? Do you list facts but forget to show how each is relevant to the law ideas? Do you list facts but forget to sequence them either in terms of importance or chronology? Do you sequence facts in a chronology but forget to identify which ideas are really crucial to the success of the argument?

Language mistakes like this are indications of dithering at the thinking stage. In Chapter 8, you will be introduced to a tool to help you choose the right language. But first a tool to clarify your thinking might help.

6.3.3   Dithering at the problem phase: a checklist

If you find that some of your written arguments from the past contain some of these flaws, or if you have a problem that you are presently trying to resolve and you are stuck, it is helpful to try to track your thinking process at the conscious level. De Bono's book *The Five Day Course in Thinking* helps you do this with a set of practical exercises (De Bono (1967)).

Once you have articulated the pattern of the relationships between the facts and the law issues, you will be able to work out whether you are drawing conclusions based on authority, language or logic. You will be in a position to assess your conclusions in the solution analysis phase (Chapter 7).

The checklist for problem analysis (figure 6.1) sets out trigger expressions to help you describe:

- the applicable laws you find in research;
- the status and authority of those laws;
- the facts;
- the status and authority of those facts;
- the argument that relates the facts to the laws or the laws to each other;
- the certainty with which you have reached a conclusion.

PROBLEM ANALYSIS

AND YOU:

9. CONTRACT THE LIST BY DELETING INAPPLICABLE ITEMS OR PATTERNING REMAINING ITEMS

BECAUSE

10. OF AUTHORITY THAT IS:

11.
- ☐ obiter,
- ☐ ratio,
- ☐ express,
- ☐ implied,
- ☐ binding,
- ☐ persuasive,
- ☐ common law,
- ☐ statute

12. RECONCILING STATUS ARGUMENTS

13. OF COURTS
- ☐ binding,
- ☐ persuasive,
- ☐ single judgment,
- ☐ multiple judgment,
- ☐ majority,
- ☐ dissent,
- ☐ top of hierarchy,
- ☐ bottom of hierarchy

14. OF STATUTES
statute, regulation, bye-law

OR RETURN TO SITUATION APPRAISAL

15. USING FACTS THAT ARE
- ☐ relevant,
- ☐ admissible,
- ☐ weighty,
- ☐ persuasive

16. USING LANGUAGE IN
- ☐ common,
- ☐ specialist,
- ☐ dictionary,
- ☐ legal -case law
- ☐ legal -statute,
- ☐ express or implied MEANINGS

17. AS LOGICAL ARGUMENT

18. NOMINATING FACT OR LAW AS
- ☐ conditions,
- ☐ necessary,
- ☐ sufficient,
- ☐ necessary & sufficient

19. ENTAILING CONCLUSIONS

20.
- ☐ deductively,
- ☐ inductively,
- ☐ analogically
- ☐ persuasively (as rhetoric)

21.
- ☐ right,
- ☐ probably right,
- ☐ more probable than not,
- ☐ 49%-51% etc.

22. TO PLACE POSSIBLE SOLUTIONS ON THE ACTION LIST

 **CONTRACTIONARY MODE**

Figure 6.1

> **WHEN YOU ANALYSE THE LAW ISSUES YOU:**

1. THE LIST OF POSSIBLE ITEMS TO CONSIDER

   BY

2. **LISTING AUTHORITY FOR**

3. **FACTS THAT ARE:**
   relevant, persuasive, have weight, admissible
   ❑ by eye witness
   ❑ by documents
   ❑ by expert opinion
   ❑ as original evidence
   not excluded by hearsay

4. **RELATING TO LAW THAT IS:**
   ❑ policy,
   ❑ principle,
   ❑ a rule,
   ❑ an exception,
   ❑ a qualification,
   ❑ express,
   ❑ implied,
   ❑ statute,
   ❑ common law,
   ❑ private agreement

5. **USING LANGUAGE THAT**
   ❑ defines,
   ❑ describes,
   ❑ exemplifies,
   ❑ acts as analogy or metaphor,
   ❑ qualifies,
   ❑ adds,
   ❑ compares or contrasts,

6. **AS LOGICAL ARGUMENT THAT MIGHT**
   ❑ define,
   ❑ negate,
   ❑ support,
   ❑ corroborate,
   ❑ contradict,
   ❑ rebut,
   ❑ conclude

7. **AND BY THINKING CREATIVELY AND HOLISTICALLY**

8. **TO REACH A TENTATIVE CONCLUSION IN LAW**

◀▮▮▮▮▮▶ **EXPANSIONARY MODE**

The trigger expressions ask you first to identify precise expressions for the kind of authority, language and argument you think might support your tentative conclusion. The process of reaching a tentative conclusion is an expansionary thinking mode, when adding (ie coordinating) ideas to your list.

The trigger expressions ask you secondly to identify precise expressions for the kind of authority, language, and logical arguments you will rely on to draw a conclusion. This is a process of decision making that requires you to give reasons for deleting and to design patterns for organising the ideas on your list. This process of decision making is a contractionary thinking mode, when deleting or patterning (ie subordinating) ideas.

The trigger expressions are designed to help you have a clear conversation with yourself about your process of thinking in relation to the law issues. If you do this, you will also be able to compare your first thoughts with the file's ultimate legal solution. This will help you learn from experience and avoid the bias with hindsight that the ultimate answer was what you thought all along (Kahneman (1982) and see also Chapter 2). Chapter 7 contains a further device to help the client rank solutions. Chapter 8 contains a dithering device to help you choose the right words so that you can have a clear conversation with someone else.

Let's apply the problem analysis checklist to the case of 'A roof over their heads'. You might start with the thought that the original investment may be unenforceable by reason of the breach of provisions of the relevant company law.

When expanding this thought, you might

• List authority

(a) in the form of relevant persuasive and admissible facts

(b) relating the facts to statute law whose provisions amount to a set of rules

(c) to which there are some exceptions to the rules that must be checked

(d) case law further helps define the circumstances in which those rules apply

- Use language that defines, describes and give examples
- Develop logical argument that defines and corroborates your tentative conclusion that the offer should have been accompanied by a prospectus and rebuts any counter arguments.

When drawing conclusions about that argument in contractionary mode, you might think that your conclusion is correct on the following grounds:

- Authority

(a) argument rests on statute and case law that is binding, based on facts that are relevant admissible, weighty and persuasive

- Language is used expressly in its legal meaning through case law and statute
- Logical argument

(a) nominates admissible facts as necessary and sufficient

(b) argues deductively

(c) points to a conclusion that the original scheme should have been supported by a prospectus

(d) has a high probability of being correct in law. You would have deleted any items added to your list in contractionary mode that did not satisfy these standards.

At any time in thinking through a legal problem, you might discover that your argument is flawed. You will return to the beginning of the problem analysis phase and start again. In some problems, you might even need to return to the beginning of the situation appraisal phase.

You may now apply some further expansionary and contradictory techniques, as appropriate to clarify your thinking in problem analysis. Some examples of these techniques and suggestions for how to use them are set out below.

6.4   Expansionary thinking in problem analysis

6.4.1   Inductive logic

Definition and example

Induction is one of the processes of formal logic. Formal logic and deduction are discussed in more detail in para 6.5.3. Induction involves the process of drawing a wider inference from a number of pieces of information which themselves are often narrower and are not necessarily related. If you were a spy, you might report:

Fact one   All soldiers have been recalled from leave

Fact two   All vehicles have been commandeered by the state

Fact three   Citizens have been told to listen to the 6.00pm broadcast each evening.

Your superiors might draw the inference that their enemy State was on red alert, in preparation for an attack. In an inductive inference the conclusion is at a higher level of generality that the facts given. More general language is used in the conclusion than in the premises.

In medicine and law

Physicians use induction every time they diagnose the disease based on the symptoms you relate. The most famous case of induction in common law is the case of *Donoghue v Stevenson*. In that case, Lord Atkin declared that the neighbour principle explained the damages awarded in a number of quite different factual situations.

In science, induction often involves reasoning from effects back to causes. In law, induction often involves reasoning from highly concrete language to more abstract language. Lord Atkin listed the facts of the cases in which compensation had been paid in concrete detail and then declared the neighbour principle to be the overarching principle that linked them together. Research suggests that problem solvers find it harder to reason from effect back to cause (Kahneman (1982)). Perhaps lawyers also find it harder to reason with language at different levels of generality and abstraction. The more abstract the language in which an argument is couched, the harder it is to use common sense, fact and personal experience to act as a check on the solution.

Only the higher courts tend to use induction often. They use it to declare a new or amended principle of law. Such cases tend to involve large amounts of money or very important issues of principle for a client. The private client will need a lot of money or will need to be supported by the State to take such a case to the highest tribunal.

The lower the court, the more likely the decision will be based closely on the facts and on an agreed statement of the existing law. The reasoning, therefore, in coming to a conclusion will be more likely to be deductive. The higher the court, the more it is possible to hope for a focus on principle rather than fact. Indeed, in the case of *Donoghue v Stevenson*, the existence of the snail in the bottle was never required to be proven and counsel for the defendant is reported to have sworn to the end of his days that no such snail ever existed!

Analogy

Analogy is thought by some commentators to be a form of induction. Where there are sufficient points of similarity that cover both the necessary and sufficient conditions to suggest a similar conclusion, then there will be an analogy between two cases on the statement of the law. Even where the statement of law is not authoritative, similar facts offer a fund of vicarious human experience that might justify the same conclusion. The judge will try hard to argue around difficulties in legal reasoning. Although lower courts would rarely decide a case by declaring a new principle reached inductively, they will often make decisions as analogy between similar facts based on the view that similar facts should condition similar outcomes.

Sometimes arguments are understood as deductive arguments but are meant as analogies. An argument that abortion is punishable as murder may not be a valid deductive argument, but might be quite forceful as an analogy. The difficulty is that when presented as a conclusion, the listener does not know the basis upon which the argument is to be judged. When presented as a conclusion, the problem solver cannot view the problem from the perspective of the other side unless he or she teases out the basis of the argument, the meaning of the language, etc.

6.4.2 The narrative

'See what Bedingfield has done to me' cried the victim in the case that was to become *R v Bedingfield* when she came out of the room with her throat cut and died shortly after.

The law of evidence admits evidence that would otherwise be excluded by operation of the hearsay rule under the rule of the *res gestae* (things done). Statements will be admissible as part of the *evidence* because they are thought to be relevant on account of their contemporaneity with matters under investigation (Byrne QC in *Cross on Evidence*(1986)).

Here, the plaintiff cry of the victim was not admitted as part of the *evidence* because Cockburn LJ decided that the relevant act was over. If she had said, 'Don't, Harry' while her throat was being cut that would have been admissible. It was not even admissible as a dying declaration because it was not clear if the victim had a settled and hopeless expectation of death!

Apart from the fascination for generations of law students that the fine distinctions drawn in *R v Bedingfield* have held, narrative is not much used in the classroom as a teaching device, but in life the story is not complete without the conversation and the pictures that enliven understanding and sharpen recall (Bair (1984)).

Chapter 2 (at para 2.3.1) outlined research demonstrating the relative superiority of narrative as a persuasive device over statistical evidence of probabilities. Obtaining a successful result in a court proceeding will rely on skilful direction of the story. If it is an ancient tale of rage or lust or pain, certain community beliefs and stereotypes are hard to fight. Helena Kennedy's book about the depiction of women and minorities in British courts gives some startling examples of success and failure in this regard (Kennedy (1992)).

Advocates use the expression 'the theory of the case' to express the idea that the role of the advocate is to hone and focus the story so that the jury can grasp that why and the what in a simple statement (see *Advocacy* by Andy Boon in this series at para 3.5).

A narrative will include the colourful language, the irrelevancies, the digressions, the irrelevant motivations and intentions, the irrelevant opinions and the jumbled sequence that is characteristic of most people's recall. These are the items solicitors remove from their version to the client or to counsel confirming the facts. Yet it is precisely these narrative elements that are so useful in identifying motive. Motive is at the heart of many criminal complaints. It is also relevant in assessing the credibility and acceptability of witness' statements. Twining notes the importance of narrative in the sentencing, if not in the resolution of the legal questions (Twining (1990))

A narrative is by definition an account of what happened from the perspective of one person at a time. The narrative accounts overlap, corroborate, contradict and reveal gaps. The existence of an incomplete story gives the story itself veracity. Given the imperfection of memory, a story told too well and in too much detail many days after the event is likely to have grown or become distorted in the telling (see also Chapter 3).

Even a commercial transaction thought to be dry and routine will have aspects of narrative. The client's expectations and objectives are bound up in hopes for success and concerns for risk. A client in middle management in a large commercial organisation has aspirations for promotion that lurk in the background of the instructions. A fear of explaining large lawyer's fees to one's manager is a greater motivation for cautious instructions than the young lawyer might appreciate.

6.4.3   The best, worst case

The problem that you are trying to solve has undoubtedly been posed before with some variation. It is always helpful to know if your case is typical (in which problem definitions and their solutions from the past are likely to apply without much modification). If your case is unusual the differences might themselves turn the statement of the problem into something quite different from other cases, requiring different or new solutions.

How you rank the case in relation to others (best, worst) will be of significance to the Action issue as well as to the legal issues. For example, in some jurisdictions, once the patent period expired extensions were granted only on application to the court showing a worthy case. In pharmaceutical patents, the case often came down to the fact that the drug was patented many years before human trials were completed and long before the drug was authorised for sale. Unless the court extended the patent period, so the argument went, the patent owner would have no opportunity to exploit its commercial monopoly and to recoup its investment. The period granted in extension was related to the court's assessment of the merits of the claim. Therefore, when acting for a drug company likely to be seeking a number of patent extensions each year, the ability to assess those cases likely to be regarded by the court as extraordinary (and therefore worthy of the maximum extension) as opposed to ordinary cases (entitled to enjoy a lesser extension) was of some practical importance. If the advocate pitches the worth of a case too high, then the judge is less likely to accept that argument in subsequent cases.

6.4.4   Creative possibilities

Creative techniques in problem solving in business usually help the problem solver see the facts or problem in a new light. At the problem analysis stage, the lawyer can ask:

- what would I do if the matter involved much more money or much less money?
- what could the client do if the client had no legal representation?
- how would other client advisors (merchant bankers, accountants, risk analysts) define this problem?
- what might these other advisors do about the problem?
- what would happen if the client did nothing, or did nothing for a time?

In medicine, as in law, doing nothing for a time can sometimes affect the problem in surprisingly positive ways. Creative problem solving techniques also ask the problem solver to define the problem in ways other than the strictly analytical. Define it as a motto from the client's point of view and then as a motto from the point of view of the other side. Summarise the problem in a picture or a popular song. These techniques might only be helpful in the occasional case, but the focus they bring to that case will be very generative for problem analysis.

6.5   Contractionary thinking tools in problem analysis

6.5.1   Climate change checklist

A first essential step either in entering problem analysis or before leaving it is to ask if anything has changed since the last time you considered the problem. Often the situation appraisal phase will take place in the presence of the client at a first interview. The problem analysis phase takes place in earnest when the client leaves and you begin to research the law and make a decision about further facts needed or evidence to be taken. You need to keep your mind open to change. Have the facts, law, your own, the firm's, or the client's situation changed slightly or dramatically since the last time you looked at the problem?

6.5.2 Venn diagrams

John Venn was a 19th century logician who invented a means of representing relationship between categories so that the relationships of inclusion, exclusion and overlap could be represented pictorially. The doodle pads of many lawyers show the use of Venn diagrams in legal reasoning. They are an excellent aid to group problem solving, since pictorial representation can be understand at a glance and remembered more easily.

Venn diagrams can be used as a first step in problem analysis when the problem is to redraft a document into plain English. Take, for, example, this clause from a Request for Further and Better Particulars:

> 'In this Request wherever "the usual particulars" are sought of any agreement, say whether the same was wholly or partly in writing or to be implied. In so far as the same was in writing, identify sufficiently each document constituting the same ... In so far as the same was oral, say when, where and between what actual persons ... In so far as the same was to be implied, set forth each act, thing, matter or circumstance, etc.'

The language of the paragraph implies that there are three possible categories of 'usual particulars', referring to each of the three sentences that follow the first. Is that correct?

In combination, at least six categories come to mind:

- express oral statement;
- implied oral statement;
- express statement from an agreement wholly in writing;
- implied statement from an agreement wholly in writing;
- express statement from an agreement partly in writing and partly oral;
- implied statement from an agreement partly in writing and partly oral.

A Venn diagram helps represent these categories. First a statement can be partly oral and partly written. These are the first two circles in the diagram (see figure 6.2).

Figure 6.2

The two categories can overlap representing a statement partly oral and partly written. The two circles are represented as overlapping (see figure 6.3).

Figure 6.3

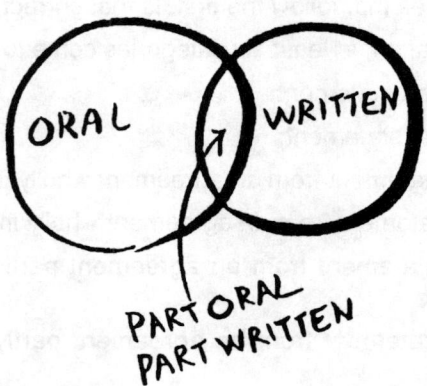

A statement can either be express or implied. These
categories are mutually exclusive, not overlapping (see figure 6.4)

Figure 6.4

There can be an express statement taken from a source partly
written and partly oral (see figure 6.5).

Figure 6.5

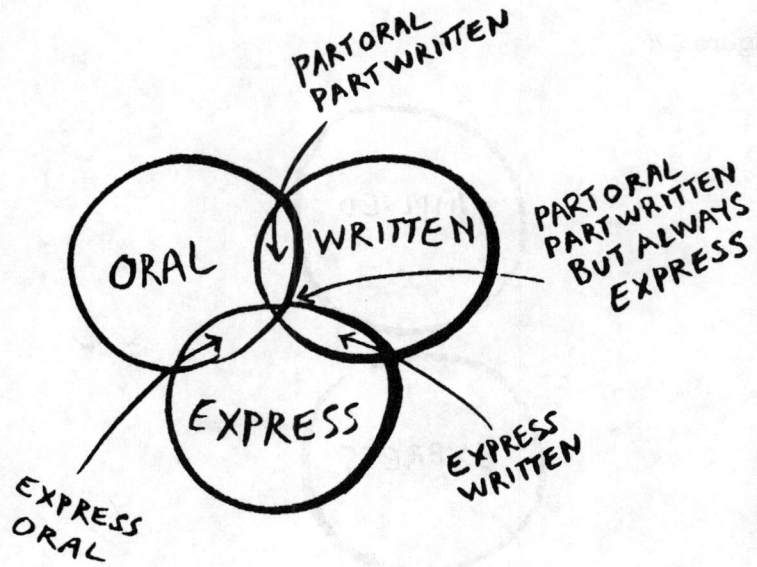

There can be an implied statement taken from a source partly written and partly oral? (See figure 6.6.)

Figure 6.6

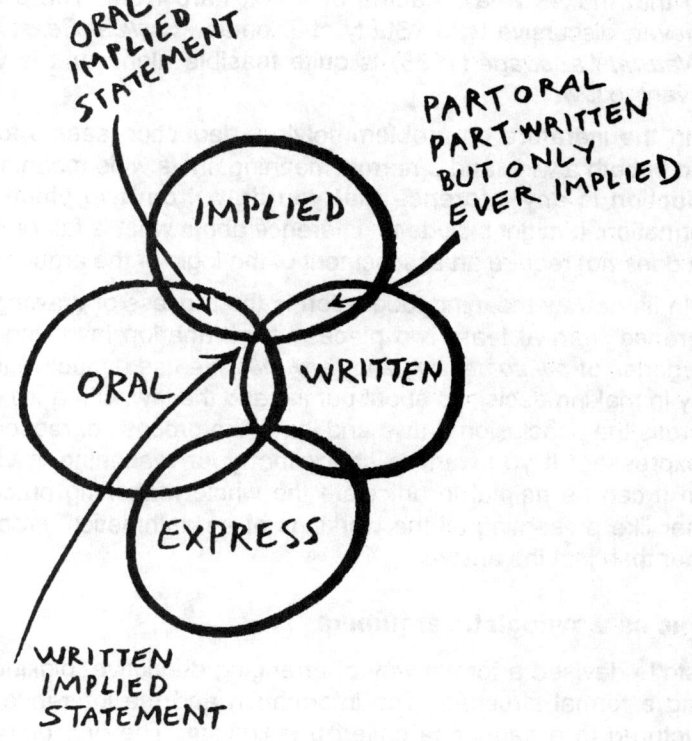

The use of Venn diagrams would enable the author, in this example, to create a plain language document asking the deponent to deal with each of the possible categories in checklist form.

6.5.3 Deductive logic

Paragraph 6.3.1 suggests that logic is one of the ways in which facts will be related to the law. Formal logic is divided into two processes: deduction, discussed here; and induction, discussed above in para 6.4.1. Formal logic has a technical language of its own that makes a lay reading of a text hard work. There are, however, discursive texts. Study of Thomas *Practical Reasoning in Natural Language* (1986) is quite feasible alone and is very relevant to law.

In the literature on problem solving, deduction seems to be used in both a wide and a narrow meaning. In its wide meaning, a deduction is any inference that you draw from two pieces of information. It might include an inference about what is fair or right that does not require an assessment of the logic of the argument.

In its narrow meaning, deduction is the process of drawing an inference from at least two pieces of information involving the categories of *all, some, are,* and (*are*) *not.* We use deductive logic daily in making decisions about our life and the law. Often we only express the conclusion drawn and leave the process of reasoning unexpressed. If you want to check that your reasoning is valid, then it can be helpful to articulate the whole reasoning process, rather like presenting all the workings of an arithmetical problem rather than just the answer.

Logic as a syllogistic argument

Aristotle devised a formal way of arranging deductive thinking by using a formal structure. The information and the inference are structured in a sequence called a syllogism. The first piece of information is called *a major premise*, the second *a minor premise*, and the inference *a conclusion*.

Valid reasoning that is true

The classic example from Aristotle is:

Major premise: All men are mortal

Minor premise: Socrates is a man

Conclusion: Therefore Socrates is mortal

If the predicate of the second premise is part of the subject of the first premise then the inference will be valid. The conclusion is at a lower level of generality than the premises and uses more specific language.

Valid reasoning, but not true

Note that inference can be valid but not true because the truth of the inference depends upon the truth of each of the premises. For example:

Major premise: All lawyers are crooks

Minor premise: Jack is a lawyer

Inference: Jack is a crook

Invalid and untrue

It is also possible to draw a false conclusion through faulty logic. The predicate of the second premise (mortals) is a wider concept that the subject of the first premise (barristers), therefore the conclusion is invalid as well as untrue.

Major premise: All barristers are human

Minor premise: All humans are mortal

Conclusion: Therefore, all mortals are barristers

This explanation merely scratches the surface of deductive logic. Further structures in categorical logic enable the problem solver to deal with negative arguments and arguments made from opposite statements and to spot some of the most common logic fallacies in argument since these are just as relevant to assessing the validity of the other side's argument at the implementation stage. This will be discussed at para 8.5.3 below.

An example

Deductive arguments are often presented as conclusions, or more insidiously, as implied conclusions only. When they speak to that part of our intuition that Posner calls presupposition (para 6.3), it can be useful to set them out as formal syllogisms to examine both the existence of the facts upon which the conclusions are based, their truth and the logic of the conclusion drawn. Take the following conclusion:

All abortion should be punished as murder.

Articulating the argument in the form of a syllogism enables each premise to be examined for truth and each conclusion to be examined for truth and logic. The syllogism would look something like this:

Major premise: All murder is unlawful

Minor premise: Abortion is murder

Conclusion: Therefore, abortion is unlawful and should be punished as murder

In this case, the first premise is true. The truth of the second premise is a question of language in law; is *abortion* included in the definition of *murder*? In most jurisdictions, it is not. It fails, therefore, as a valid deductive argument. It might remain valid as a statement of what the law should be, but that requires a different argument.

Another example

The special rules of evidence applicable to crimes of rape are often justified on the basis that rape is a charge easy to make out and hard to defend. The truth of this premise remained unchallenged until recently. The logical conclusion from the facts is that, therefore, the special rules are justifiable. Helena Kennedy (1992) points out that the premise is not true: rape is a charge that women find very difficult to make and that there is substantial evidence of underreporting. She asserts that, from her experience at least, rape is a fairly easy charge to defend.

Further structures for logic

There is another kind of deductive logic, thought to be even more important than categorical logic. Propositional logic deals with the logical terms *not, or, and, if then*. Here is a typical legal argument formulated in terms of propositional logic.

If a will is

- in writing
- validly witnessed
- by a testator of sound mind
- subject to no duress

then, the will be valid and enforceable.

There is no longer an absolute relationship between subjects and predicates, but a conditional relationship between two sets of statements. In law, we often deal with situations in which certain conditions need to be present to allow for a particular conclusion. In law, hard cases are often hard because the judge is called upon to identify the minimum conditions that allow for that particular legal conclusion. This question in logic is expressed as whether conditions are *necessary, sufficient* or *necessary and sufficient*. Only a condition that is necessary and sufficient will always result in a particular conclusion.

Applying a legal illustration to each of these terms will show their utility for lawyers in thinking.

A necessary condition is one that must be present but that alone does not conclude the argument. For example:

If Mrs Smith has made a will

Mrs Smith is of sound mind

Then, is the will valid?

Testamentary capacity is one of the conditions necessary to a valid will, but not the only condition. If the will is not validly executed or if Mrs Smith were subject to duress, then the will would not be valid in spite of her testamentary capacity.

A sufficient condition for a state of affairs, if it exists, will logically result in a particular conclusion. But that conclusion does not always have to be reached by the existence of that condition. For example:

If there is duress, then the will will be invalid.

The existence of duress is sufficient to result in invalidity but not necessary. Invalidity can also be present if, for example, the testator was of unsound mind.

A condition can be both **necessary and sufficient.** A condition that is both necessary and sufficient will result in a particular conclusion, and every time that conclusion is reached, that condition will also have to be present. To revert to the original wills example:

If the will is in writing, validly witnessed and the testator was of sound mind, then the will is valid.

The conditions of writing, witnessing and soundness of mind are together necessary and sufficient to result in the conclusion of validity. Every time that conclusion is made those conditions must exist.

The concepts of *necessary, sufficient, necessary and sufficient* are useful is assessing the evidence in any given case against the authorities. For example, in a case of negligent misstatement, the existence of an inaccurate statement is necessary but not sufficient, since it is essential to show reliance on the statement and loss causally flowing from the reliance. In a case of manufacturer's negligence, the presence of a deteriorating snail in a bottle of ginger beer that causes injury, will be a sufficient condition but is not necessary (the injury could be caused by other forms of contamination in the contents or on the bottle).

In a statutory case of driving under the influence, it may be both a necessary and a sufficient condition for the police to produce a certificate that the accused was found to have a reading of .05 alcohol or more in his or her bloodstream when tested by the authorised equipment. Evidence that the accused was actually not impaired by the consumption of alcohol in the performance of certain tasks (such as walking a straight line) formerly given to test impairment would then be irrelevant.

These concepts are also relevant in trying to define the ratio of the case. Judges often say more about ideas that are wrong than ideas that are right. Judges comment more about factors that are not sufficient than factors that are not necessary. If a factor is both necessary and sufficient and present in the case, it is often passed over without comment at all. In construing the ratio, it can be helpful to summarise factors that appear to be both necessary and sufficient to result in a particular conclusion, because this is the minimum evidence required in future cases. To do this, you will need to read the facts carefully and even the notes of argument sometimes found at the beginning of reports.

Logic arguments and language arguments

Deductive arguments are closely related to arguments about language. Arguments in both categorical and propositional logic rely on the acceptance that certain asserted facts or states of affairs are true. Language arguments can appear to be logic arguments until it is appreciated that the issue is not truth, or the validity of inference, but the meaning of language. The argument about abortion being unlawful (above) is actually an argument about language.

Untangling arguments about authority, logic and language

Arguments about language or about authority are often presented in law as arguments about logic. When the question is asked whether the right of a purchaser of land under a contract of sale is an *insurable interest*, three kinds of questions are being asked. First, as a question of authority, what kinds of interests have been held to be insurable interests in the past. Second, as a question of language meaning, what meanings does the expression insurable interest have in the dictionary and the market place. Third, as a question of logic, what minimum conditions in the present facts (either necessary, sufficient or necessary and sufficient) must be shown to exist for an interest to be regarded as insurable when reasoning on the basis of authority and language?

Language arguments put forward as syllogistic reasoning are often seen as overly legalistic and arid. Yet it was this form of argument that Portia used to save her lover from Shylock.

Take then thy bond, take thou thy pound of flesh,
But, in cutting it, if thou dost shed
One drop of Christian blood, thy lands and goods
Are, by the laws of Venice, confiscate
Unto the State of Venice.
From *The Merchant of Venice*, Act 1V, Scene 1

If you find it hard to reduce your argument to writing convincingly, it can be help to try to untangle the threads of the argument. Characterise elements of your argument so that you know which is about language, which about authority and which about logic. Try using the checklist in figure 6.1.

6.5.5 Chronology

Establishing a time order for actions in the past or steps to be taken in the future can be helpful.

In disputes over what has happened in the past, a chronology of events should be taken at the outset. It is easier to note inconsistencies, omissions, overstatement, unexplained conduct if you can run the events through in your mind like a film.

The drafting of pleadings is assisted by reference to a chronological statement of events. An important problem relevant to the Action issue is whether to settle or whether to go to trial. An ordered statement of the matters upon which evidence must be adduced enables a systematic list of all the evidence needed and an assessment of the weight credibility and cost of proof. Cost and risk are always relevant elements in the Action issue.

The recitals of facts in judgments can be deceptive. Often they are not stated in chronological order or only events thought to be relevant to the final decision are listed.

Take, for example, the case *In Re Vandervell's Trusts (No 2)* [1974] 1 Ch 269. The judgment on appeal dealt with the narrow question of who was beneficially entitled to a certain parcel of 100,000 shares. It was of some practical importance because on one view the shares would have been subject to considerable surtax. The facts describing the complex trust arrangement are set out, but the reasons for this arrangement are not given. If your curiosity is piqued as to why Mr Vandervell arranged his affairs in that particular way, you need to read two lines of cases back to the original application and piece together all the facts and underlying motivations.

6.5.6   Visual aids to problem analysis

There is a trend to use of all kinds of visual representation in legal practice. In litigation involving complex facts, a flowchart setting out each party's version of events and the interpretation to be placed on them in law can simplify the presentation of the case. The judge can be presented with a party's complete argument in opening submissions. The trial actually becomes a process of selection between alternate pictures of the issues. The role of evidence, in effect, becomes to corroborate or to contradict one party's version of the story.

Where your problem is a drafting one and you are seeking to express a process or procedure to take place in the future, classification tables, flowcharts and time lines are other useful ways of clarifying time relationships for you, the thinker. They also have the handy feature of being clear implementation devices as well.

Relationship diagrams

Both litigious and commercial cases can involve many parties. Perhaps the commercial deal involves a company structure of more than 20 companies with interlocking shareholding. Perhaps the case is a class action involving more than 100 suits for damages for personal injury for defective saline breast implants, sharing common questions of liability but subject to different hearings on quantum. You can imagine that a consideration of even some of the issues involving the Lloyd's difficulties in the London insurance market would be impossible without a diagram.

Diagrams are used increasingly in the legal environment. No common conventions seem to be adhered to in their preparation. It is therefore important that all people using the diagram have it explained by the author and have a descriptive text of its meaning to which they can refer. With that limitation, a diagram is a formalised mind map of the relationship between parties. You are more likely to be able to retain more than nine items of information expressed as a diagram (see *Legal Writing* by Margot Costanzo in this series at para 2.4.5) than if the relationships are merely expressed in text.

If you are unable to draw a diagram of the relationship between the parties, it might be because you are lacking some facts.

Flowcharts of events

A diagram is a depiction of relationships frozen as at one point in time. One analogy would be with a balance sheet, a financial statement that shows assets and liabilities as at a certain date. A flowchart, on the other hand, shows the dynamic relationship between parties as it changes over time. The financial analogy with a flowchart is the profit and loss account that shows whether a profit or loss was made over a given period of time. If you cannot prepare a flowchart for events, it might mean that you still have investigations about facts or above motives and reasons to complete. If your problem is to set out procedural steps clearly in a flowchart, difficulty in preparing the flowchart might require a return to Law issues for clarification.

A special flowchart – Wigmorean analysis

Wigmore developed a technique for charting the facts in issue and the law in a trial. He illustrated this technique by reference to cases that had already been solved, and so I do not know if any advocate during Wigmore's lifetime actually used the technique in preparation for trial, in argument or for summing up.

In an era where colour printing was extremely expensive, his charting technique involved a set of intricate symbols designed to distinctively represent evidence of each party, whether corroborating or contradicting relative to the legal arguments to be made. The technique requires considerable time to master. Apart from the rigorous knowledge of the law required to present an accurate chart, the number of symbols would require constant use with rigorous review before they became known by rote.

Terence Anderson and William Twining have adapted and improved upon Wigmore's techniques for charting (Gold et al (1989)). The adoption of colour and shading would assist in reducing the relatively large number of symbols to be mastered. This charting technique is also ripe for transfer to a computer program and would be more suitable for adaptation to the law than the general flowcharting programs used increasingly by large law firms.

The power of visual representation also leaves open the possibility of distortion and confusion unless some rules for the representation of facts are followed. Take a complex case in which there are many payments of money between the alleged thief and the alleged fence in a stolen car racket. Like payments should be given like symbols. Each symbol must be rigorously backed by evidence of sufficient probative value and weight to justify the classification that the use of the symbol implies. This technique requires rigorous rules for symbol choice and depiction of relationships similar to the rules for language dealing with diction and syntax.

Examination of the techniques of Anderson and Twining techniques will repay the effort many times over. You will certainly examine the facts and the law with greater rigour than textual examination alone would ever require. Even if you decide that a particular case does not warrant the time that a complete chart would require, this charting technique can be used as a kind of fund of ideas for the ways in which you might depict your client's particular story on one page.

6.5.7   A fourway problem definition

Ned Herrmann suggests that all problems should be given four definitions (Herrmann (1990)). This fourway definition will require you to wear all of De Bono's hats. Applying this suggestion to the professional negligence possibility in the case of 'The roof over their heads', the classes of definition, with examples would be as follows:

- A rational definition

Has the clients' accountant breached his fiduciary duty to the clients in giving advice about their entering a scheme in which he had a financial interest? (You could go on to list the necessary and sufficient conditions that have to be satisfied to prove this claim and to assess each piece of evidence in the light of what is required.)

- A detailed chronological prioritised definition

The steps in proceedings to litigate this question of fiduciary duty (you might list steps in accordance with the procedural requirements of the jurisdiction) would be:

- A personalised definition

of what it means from the perspective of each of the people involved.

The clients would say that success in this claim will mean that they can resume their normal lives and dare to hope again. From the accountant's point of view, this claim might amount to professional and personal humiliation or it might only be a glitch in his normal practice.

• A conceptual overview of the big picture

The question of breach of fiduciary duty is only one head of the client's claim and should be viewed alongside the other two possible actions.

6.6   Summary of problem analysis

The problem analysis phase encompasses the research and legal analysis questions so familiar to law students. It also requires a rigorous and pragmatic investigation of both the facts and the client's objectives, issues in which the law student has had little practice. In the expansionary mode of thinking you will have added many more matters of detail to the list. In the contractionary mode you will have devised patterns to relate the items to each other as well as having eliminated irrelevant items of fact and law. You will have added to the Action list a number of other possibilities.

6.7   End of chapter references and additional reading

Anderson, Terence
Twining, William
(1991)
Analysis of Evidence Weidenfeld
Paperbooks

Baier, Paul R
(1984)
What is the use of a law book without pictures or conversations 34 Jo of Legal Education 619

Bourke, Judy
(1993)
Misapplied Science Unreliability in Scientific Test Evidence 10 Aust Bar Review 123

Byrne, D W QC
Heydon, J D QC
(1986)
Cross on Evidence Butterworths

Cross, Rupert
(1969)
The Periphery of Hearsay 7 MULR 1

de Bono, Edward
(1967)
The Five Day Course in Thinking Basic
Books

Gold, Neil
Mackie, Karl
Twining, William(ed)
(1989)
Learning Lawyer's Skills Butterworths

Herrmann, Ned
(1990)
The Creative Brain Lake Lure

Kahneman, David
Slovic, Paul
Tversky, Amos
(1982)
*Judgment under uncertainty: Heuristics
and biases* Cambridge University Press

Kennedy, Helena QC
(1992)
*Eve was framed: Women and British
Justice* Chatto Windus London

Posner, Richard A
(1990)
The Problems of Jurisprudence Harvard
University Press

Thomas, Stephen
Naylor
(1986)
Practical Reasoning in Natural Language
Prentice Hall 3rd edition

Twining, William
(1990)
Rethinking Evidence
Blackwell, Oxford

Twining, William
(1989)
Reading Law 24 Valparaiso University
Law Review 1

7 Solution Analysis

What judgment shall I dread, doing no wrong?

Shylock, The Merchant of Venice, Act IV, Scene I

The Lawyer as Creator

7.1 Solution analysis: three questions for the Action issue

If Shylock had been living in this century, with a television, he would have known that there are risks inherent to litigation even when the litigant has done no wrong. For every client, whether litigious or commercial, there will be costs in taking legal action, even if only in their time. Risk is one side of the solution analysis coin. Benefit is the other side.

At the solution analysis phase, you need to do two things. First, you need to check that the Action list is complete. Perhaps there are simpler and quicker solutions to the problem than traditional legal solutions. Second, you need to help the client define benefit, risk and cost so that the client can make a decision about what to do with full information. He or she will make the decision. But nothing is so tidy. As in the other phases, you might start to analyse the actions but quickly realise that you have made a mistake in constituting the facts or in conceiving one of the logic, language or authority arguments from which your solution list was derived (see Chapter 6). Even at the solution phase, you might find that you need to backtrack in the problem solving process and re-think solution appraisal.

By the time you have reached the solution analysis phase, the focus will be on questions for the Action issue. There still remains the quick check on the Threshold issue that there has been no change. You will also keep a sharp eye out for changes affecting facts. The Law issue will still be relevant in two ways.

First, it will be relevant if you discover during solution analysis that you have made a mistake in the authority, logic or language arguments that are the foundation of the legal conclusion. In that case you might need to go back to the beginning of the problem analysis phase. In some cases you might even need to return to the situation analysis phase.

Second, if the solution analysis concludes with your client deciding to adopt a course which involves following a highly regulated legal procedure, you might find that there are law issues involved in working out how the procedure should be implemented. This throws up a narrower law issue that should be investigated by returning to situation analysis.

In considering the Action issue, there are three major questions to be answered:

- What are the client's goals?

- What is the probability that any legal solution will achieve the client's goals?

- On a comparison of benefits for the client in achieving the goal versus the costs and the risks, which solution should the client choose?

If situation analysis is like the big cat sniffing the air to find the right path and problem analysis is like the helicopter turning the spotlight on the gang to find the ringleader, then in solution analysis you are showing the client how to operate the scales in order to weigh in the possible solutions.

Adopting an expansionary approach, you will be adding other possible items to the Action list, including actions other than those suggested by pure legal analysis. In the contractionary mode, you will be selecting, analysing and ranking possible solutions to make recommendations to the client.

7.1.1 Getting to solution analysis: a recapitulation

In the situation analysis phase (Chapter 5), we investigated the problem under four issues: Threshold, Fact, Law and Action. In considering the Threshold issue, we ascertained that we may act, and noted features about the client and ourselves relevant to our personal interaction to bear in mind for the whole transaction. In the Fact issue, we had a preliminary look at sources of information, likely witnesses, wrong factual assumptions and potential problems of proof. For the Law issue, we calibrated the dimensions of the problem and formed a hypothesis for investigation in law. For the Action issue, we noted what the client preferred and noted a few items for the list that our preliminary assessment of the Law issue revealed.

In the problem analysis phase (Chapter 5), we continued our thinking under the general headings of Threshold, Fact, Law and Action. The Threshold issue was quickly disposed of by ensuring that there has been no change since the last time we thought about the client's problem. In considering the Law issue, we validated and expanded the hypothesis formed in situation analysis by defining the facts and law in language that enabled us to make arguments about authority and meaning, and to draw valid conclusions in logic and law. We might have found at any time in the problem analysis phase that we had not defined the problem correctly, and in which case we would need to return to situation analysis and start again.

7.1.2   The lawyer wearing hat and shoes

In the solution analysis phase, Kolb suggests that we are taking on the role of inventor. Although you can be creative at the situation analysis and problem analysis phases, you will be most admired for creativity that is evident in the solution phase.

During the solution analysis phase, you will be wearing the black hat to speculate on what might be wrong about the solution, the yellow hat to identify what might be right and the green to find lateral and creative approaches perhaps not used before. You will also need the orange gumboots for legal problem solving often deals with everyday facts that involve risk to the client and even a so-called 'standard solution' will usually have to be modified.

7.2   Law in solution analysis

Case 7(A)

Smith and Fogg, a high street firm of solicitors, were delighted when judgment was handed down by the court. They had sued on a guarantee agreement which they had attempted, unsuccessfully, to activate, purchased on 30 days' credit. The guarantee was a simple, clear document guaranteeing payment by a hotelier to a consortium of liquor suppliers for the purchase price of wholesale liquor. From time to time the members of the consortium changed. The guarantee was addressed to 'Each and every member of the Wine and Spirits Association' and saved the association the trouble of having fresh guarantees executed every time the membership of the association changed. In the definition section of the guarantee it was made clear that this expression included each and every member at the time of signing the guarantee, and as constituted from time to time. ('Well, that was a fine piece of plain language drafting, even if I say so myself,' said Mr Fogg proudly.)

Naturally, Mr Fogg didn't feel that the debtor had much of a case in arguing that the guarantee was void for uncertainty. The court agreed that its meaning was certain and entered judgment for the whole of the debt. Unfortunately, the next day the judgment debtor petitioned for winding up on the grounds of insolvency. There would be no money to pay the judgment. ('Well, that was a pyrrhic victory', said the client wryly.)

Clients fear funding such a case where they win in law but lose in life. There is always the doubt that they might have been better off funding a private investigator to chase assets rather than a lawyer to chase judgment. Clarifying what the law says or means is often not the real answer to the client's problem.

'Law' is a complex concept that means different things to different people. 'Law' will also mean different things to the same practitioner depending on the client's objectives or needs. These objectives may change subtly during the course of a transaction, often depending at which stage the client consults you. Sometimes what the client should or might do is clear from the text of the law. More often, the text (for example, the guarantee agreement, above) will be just one of the many considerations in ascertaining the solution to the client's problem.

The solution analysis phase requires the lawyer to work out which version of law is to be called upon to solve the client's problem in the particular case. This is where the Law issue and the Action issue shade into one another.

7.2.1 The variety of legal solutions in solution analysis

Jurisprudential commentators tend to argue for the correctness of their definition of law to the exclusion of all other possible definitions. When it comes to seeing law as an instrument for solving problems, multiple definitions are applicable. Where multiple definitions of law are possible, so are multiple solutions. Here is a list of some of the ways law can solve a problem:

- law as text accepted as authoritative by all relevant parties;
- law as argument to persuade a judge;
- law as reasons for action by a particular decision maker;
- law as a prediction of what a judge might decide;
- law as a procedure for action;
- law as a statement of penalties for non-compliance.

In case 7(A) the law would have been used by both sides to persuade the court to find for them. At the same time, Mr Fogg would have used the law as one of the factors in predicting what the court might decide.

7.3   Defining and computing benefit

You might discover a brilliant solution during your analysis of the law, but the client will only recognise its brilliance when the solution achieves the outcome he or she expects.

7.3.1   The importance of the client's goals

Case 7(B)

Billings is a very small town. Most of the children in the town attend the local primary school. All of the children in the primary school are involved in the annual production of a musical. Those adults who are not applying makeup, working lights, adjusting sound or selling refreshments attend as audience. Last year they decided to perform the musical *Rats* (about the Pied Piper of Hamlyn and based on Robert Browning's poem). One of the parents, who had just returned from a performance of *Miss Saigon* in New York and purchased a commemorative t-shirt there, suggested that they produce a fund raising t-shirt. Everyone thought it was a great idea. They planned to reproduce the picture of the rat from the cover of the score. However, one of the parents said that he thought it would be a breach of the illustrator's copyright if it were reproduced without permission.

When the parents went to a lawyer to get advice, they were told that it was technically a breach of the illustrator's copyright but since the damages were negligible and the school had no assets to speak of, they might as well go ahead. 'It's your commercial decision', said the lawyer. Now the school committee is in deadlock. The braves want to follow the lawyer's advice and get on with it. The timids think they should just find another picture. The heritage conscious want to write to Hollywood and get the illustrator's permission.

This case illustrates the difficulties that arise in obtaining instructions when different versions of law point to a range of possible solutions, not all of which are mutually exclusive. Some clients will have strong views about the underlying moral issues and will not wish to take a strictly commercial view. Others will be dissuaded from a course of action only where the law clearly prohibits what they propose and there is some likelihood of incurring a penalty.

Often, once you have completed the problem analysis phase, you will have identified a range of possible solutions to the client's problem. It is for the client to choose, based on the goals he or she seeks to achieve.

I cannot count the number of letters of advice I have seen that describe the solution as a commercial decision for the client without any analysis of whether or how each possible solution might contribute to the achievement of the client's goals. We owe it to our clients to review the basis upon which their decision will be made, although it is not our job to make the choice. If the solution does not achieve the client's goals only three things can happen: either the lawyer returns to the problem analysis phase to see the problem in a different light so that a more satisfactory solution can be generated; the client reassesses his or her goals; or the client decides that if there is a solution to his or her problem, it is not a solution offered by a lawyer.

7.3.2   Specifying client goals

Clarity in determining goals can be achieved by viewing the universe of possible goals as containing potentially only three categories – reduction of risk; increase in profit; enhancement of values that are not about risk and profit.

Risk

When a client comes to you having been charged with a criminal matter, you might be aiming to reduce the client's risk of going to jail or of having to pay a substantial fine, by having the charge dropped or by securing an acquittal. In a significant percentage of cases, the best you will be able to achieve is to ameliorate the penalty in some way.

Likewise, in a commercial deal where the role of the lawyer is to help negotiate the rights and obligations between the parties, the client uses a lawyer to reduce the risk of the matter being unenforceable and wants to capitalise on the possibility that the lawyer knows the best terms for the deal from experience of similar transactions.

It is not possible to know the client's attitude to risk unless you discuss it with him or her (in the personal situation) or unless you know something about the industry and the particular client organisation. Attitude to risk is one of the issues that should be investigated in situation analysis (Chapter 5).

Profit

Profit is a compendious expression for money and time. Commercial deals are obviously founded in profit, although the role of a lawyer is often seen by the client as one of reducing risk rather than directly contributing to increased profit. Clients will also see their own time as a cost. A lawyer can help the client increase profit on a deal by saving management time, or by altering the time for payment of money. Depending on the prevailing interest rate, a payment now will always be more profitable than a payment of the same sum in three months' time.

Values

Let's imagine your client is a mining company. It might not only want to reduce the risk of poor publicity about its activities, but might be actively concerned to restore the mining site for use as agricultural land. It would usually do so because the failure to restore might subject the company to fines or other financial penalties, or, because there was some other financial benefit, to justify the extra expenditure, such as favourable tax treatment. The client might express the decision criteria as based on non-monetary values, but you may discover that they actually make good financial sense as well.

Private individuals, on the other hand, frequently seek to achieve outcomes that are not based on a desire to reduce risk or to increase profit. A client on whose behalf you have taken a defamation action will probably regard an apology published with prominence equal to the defamatory statements as being more important than any damages. Greenpeace might have regarded the principle that the French government was forced to admit involvement of their secret service with the bombing of the Rainbow Warrior in New Zealand as being of greater importance than the conviction and internment of two of their agents.

The lawyer needs to be wary of the client who is trying to use the legal process for revenge. Clients in matrimonial disputes sometimes seek to use the court process to punish their spouse for transgressions during the marriage not strictly relevant to the disposition of the legal suit in no-fault jurisdictions. Children or those sharing the family home become the instruments of this punishment.

While the law may deal most efficiently with questions that can be reduced to financial issues of risk and profit, we should remember that the really important issues that the law addresses are those that are priceless: the liberty of the individual, or the right to seek happiness and personal fulfilment with minimum interference from the State.

7.3.3   Reconciling conflicts in goals

In some matters the client seeks to achieve outcomes that are mutually exclusive. Usually, an outcome that is high in profit might also be higher in risk. So, a client who wants a low risk/high profit solution is not always being realistic and might need to reassess his or her goals.

If the client is looking to achieve reduced risk, increased profit and to enhance other values, the client might need to adjust the degree to which the solution is expected to achieve each of these goals. A client might need to rank goals from the necessary to the desirable and then choose the solution that has the greatest probability of delivering the optimum benefit.

For example, in the case of 'A roof over their heads' (Chapter 5), the clients only came to the lawyer hoping for an extension of time to pay. After an analysis of the Law issue in the problem phase, the lawyer might feel that this solution is less than the clients should accept, and might offer three possible solutions, each ultimately involving the initiation or defence of a law suit. Each of the possible suits could increase profits and reduce risks, but might also come into conflict with clients values, since the suits involve suing their accountant.

7.4   Defining risks and costs

7.4.1   The risks

'Winner takes all' solutions

In some legal transactions, the solutions offered will result in outcomes that are either a complete success or a complete failure. For example, if your client is a physician charged with a serious criminal offence, the prosecution might offer to reduce the charge to a lesser offence provided your client pleads guilty. You feel that on a plea, the penalty would not be jail. However, your client might be more concerned about the conviction than the severity of the penalty. Your client wants a complete acquittal. In that case, the only choices offered by defending him in a court trial are, from his point of view, all or nothing; he is either acquitted or he will be convicted.

In the case of 'A roof over their heads' there is, of course, some chance that the judge will decide that a prospectus was not necessary at all or that the accountant acted entirely properly. The clients, therefore, would be obligated to continue paying the debt which by then would have accumulated a large amount of interest.

Part win, part loss solutions

Many situations offer the risk of solutions that only achieve the client's goals in part. The judge might agree with part of the client's story but not all. In the case of 'A roof over their heads', entering into the debt without a prospectus and then re-financing that debt might be held to be significant in ways that no lawyer could have predicted. The judge might decide that only part of the money need be repaid to the clients.

In commercial transactions, it is more likely that a particular solution will achieve all the client's goals. In conveyancing, you will discharge the existing mortgage, set in place the new mortgage and arrange for the transfer of the vendor's interest in your client's name.

Provisional solutions

In more complex transactions, there might be a risk that any solution achieves the client's goals only for an interim period. The solution is provisional because it operates for a time and then the law changes, or may be at some time in the future it becomes evident that it does not provide a real solution. Tax planning is an area in which solutions are provisional: it might never be examined; it might be examined on an individual basis only; it might be the subject of a whole industry examination. In complex financial transactions, in which new forms of security are developed against an incomplete and sometimes chaotic background of case and statute law, there is always a risk that the industry practice or the particular client documentation might be adjudged defective in some way at some time in the future.

Uncertainty in predicting solutions

In most civil cases involving resolutions of disputes and in many commercial matters where the lawyer is advising on the deal, there will be more than one possible solution. For each such possible solution, one will not be able to predict with certainty that the client's desired outcomes in terms of minimising risk, maximising profit and promoting values will be achieved. Whether a particular solution is all or nothing, partial or provisional, you need to factor in some allowance about the likelihood of it occurring or not.

7.4.2 The costs

Legal costs

Each of these solutions are delivered at a cost. Clients need to give some thought as to how they balance legal costs and time involved in legal proceedings.

In the case of 'A roof over their heads', the clients would have to fund the negotiations and the law suits which would probably last a number of years. Any business person or private individual always need to weigh the certainty of paying out money today, against the possibility of recovering money in the future.

Other costs

Government charges for obtaining certified information, court fees to issue legal proceedings, fees for expert medical or other reports, fees to the arbitrator or mediator, fees to specialist services to prepare databases for facilitating complex discoveries, stamp duties and government surcharges at the time of registering a transfer of property interests, are just some of the potential solution costs in addition to legal fees. The legal profession has not done a good marketing job on just how many other fees are involved in legal work, with the result that clients often think the whole bill represents money paid only to the lawyer. Often the legal fees are slight by comparison to success fees paid to the merchant banker and stamp duties paid to the government; but only the lawyer can be sued.

7.5 Comparing the benefit with risks and costs

7.5.1 Step one: with risks

Where the goals cannot be quantified in money

In some matters it is not possible to place a sufficiently accurate money value on the risks reduced, profits increased or the values promoted in a particular solution. It may even be difficult to assess the legal costs involved. One might assess the probability of achieving a particular outcome against the benefits for the client of that outcome in an intuitive thinking process expressed in comparative language. This language can be depicted as a matrix (see figure 7.1).

Figure 7.1

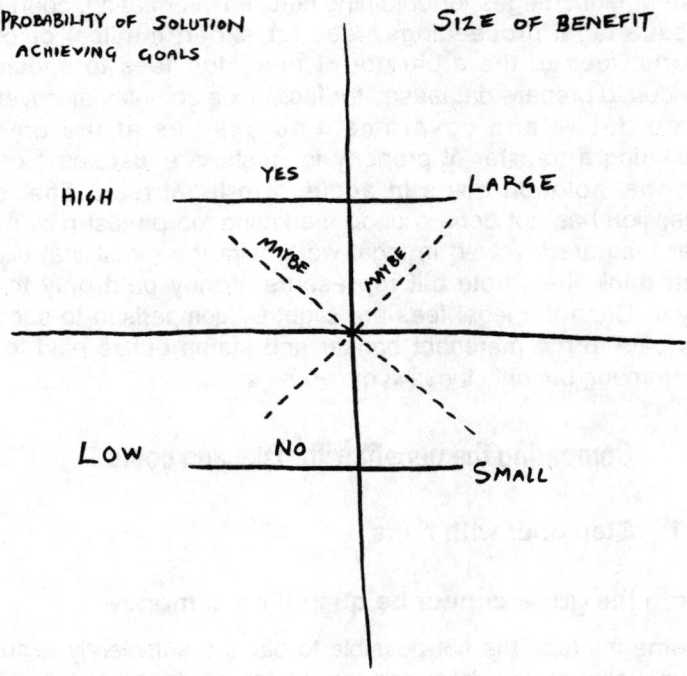

PROBABILITY BENEFITS
MATRIX

PROBABILITY OF SOLUTION   SIZE OF BENEFIT
ACHIEVING GOALS

HIGH   YES   LARGE

MAYBE   MAYBE

LOW   NO
                              SMALL

Where the relationships between these two factors (probability of achieving goals; benefit to client) in the matrix are horizontal, the assessment is simple. Where the probability of success is high and the benefits to be gained are high (as assessed by high profit or value enhancement, or a great reduction in risk) then the client will probably assess the solution as worthwhile. Conversely where probability of success is low and net benefit is low, the client will probably not pursue the solution.

Where the relationships between these two factors are diagonal the assessment is more difficult. High probabilities of success may not justify small benefits. High benefits might still justify a course of action that has a small probability of success.

Where the goals can be quantified in money

Sometimes this equation, balancing the likelihood of achieving the result against the benefit to be gained can be expressed in money. A fuller explanation of the circumstances in which this might be done and the techniques for doing it are set out below at para 7.8.2.

7.5.2   Step two: with costs

Once the client has been able to take account of the probability of goals being achieved, the last issue to weigh is legal costs.

Again, it is easier for the client to assess whether a solution is worth pursuing when the goals can be quantified and compared against likely legal costs. Specialist branches of legal practice have developed standard patterns of advice. For example, in tax planning, many practitioners will only advise entering into a particular arrangement where the legal costs of rearranging the client's affairs are recouped in tax savings in the first year of its operation. At least in those circumstances, if the revenue change regulations sometime in the future, the client might view the net result as having lost time but not money.

Where relative language is the only way of expressing the equation and the goals have a low probability of being achieved, the legal costs will be viewed as relatively high. Unless the benefit is very high, the course the client chooses will depend upon his or her attitude to risk and the ability to pay.

In these circumstances, most practitioners will want the client to deposit money on account of fees and disbursements in the trust account as a condition of acting and continuing to act.

7.6   A checklist for solution analysis

The process of adding other possible solutions in expansionary
mode, helping the client to define goals and comparing goals to
risks and costs in contractionary mode is summarised in a
checklist at figure 7.2

that make entertainment so involving and memorable are being harnessed in education to involve students and to ensure they remember what they learn.

For your client matter, it might be useful at this stage to ask how other professions might handle that or a similar problem.

A chat with another lawyer will ensure that you have not omitted any obvious solution that your client should consider. Other lawyers in other firms and other ways of dealing with the same problems in other legal systems might also give you ideas.

7.6.4   Back to brainstorming

Brainstorming is described at para 5.5.3 in Chapter 5, above.

7.7   Contractionary thinking tools for solution analysis

7.7.1   Climate change checklist

As with the other stages of problem analysis, it is always important to check features in the climate, the facts and the law to make sure that there have been no changes since the last time that you looked at the problem.

7.7.2   Computing the odds

In the process of attempting to resolve a dispute, the client will often come to the stage where the solutions to be analysed are a simple choice of whether to accept an offer that is less than their claim now, or whether to go to trial. If the client's goals in the legal transaction can be computed in money's worth, it is often worthwhile trying to assess the probability of win or loss at trial in percentage terms rather than using comparative language. It is then possible to factor in the legal costs and to compute whether a client is likely to be in a worse position for going to trial for a possible future higher benefit rather than settling for a certain present lower benefit. This calculation becomes even more important in times of high inflation.

Case 7(C): back to 'A roof over their heads'

Your original problem for these clients came down to an assessment that they could sue for the return of payments made under an invalid scheme that required a prospectus, and that they could also sue the accountant for damages for various breaches of his fiduciary duties (Chapter 5). Let us assume that at an earlier stage in problem solving, the clients analysed these possible solutions and came to the conclusion that they did not want to issue proceedings against the accountant, at least not until it could be seen whether they could get their money back from the promoter.

Assume then that the clients decided to sue the promoter for the return of the money they have paid under the original loan agreement. The promoter disputes the amount to be returned but has made an offer to settle the matter 'to get it out of the way'. Your clients are seeking £150,000. The present offer is £65,000 but you think that they will quickly come up to £80,000. The problem has now been redefined as whether your clients should settle now, or continue to sue. You have to appraise all the solutions that are possible in settling or suing.

You think that there is a 25% chance that your clients will get nothing if they go to trial because the judge will not accept your argument that a prospectus was required by law. If that is the case, then your clients will not only have to continue paying the debt, but they will also have to pay your legal costs estimated at £25,000 and a contribution to the other side's costs estimated at £15,000. That means a 25% probability of a net loss of £40,000 as opposed to the present offer of a gain of at least £65,000.

You compute the likelihood of the clients going to trial and of the judge agreeing with your version of the law at 75%. Unfortunately, it is not an all or nothing case. Your clients need to be awarded more than the present offer to take into account legal costs and time expired, to be ahead. You compute that there is a

65% chance that the judgment will beat the present offer but only a 49% chance that the judgment would exceed the £80,000 offer you think is likely. A judgment of £80,001 must be discounted by the £25,000 clients will have to pay out for legal costs. You think that there is a 75% chance that the defendants would pay out all the judgment and the £15,000 contribution to legal costs they would be required to make. You have decided on 75% because, in your experience, business people are always more anxious to pay to avoid a trial then they are to pay a judgment debt when they have lost. This still only makes a total recovery of £70,001 after legal costs have been paid.

If the judgment is less than any offer made prior to trial, the usual procedural rules as to costs will penalise the client for having run the trial. The clients will have to make a contribution to the defendants cost of running a trial. So if they get a judgment for £79,999, by the time your clients have paid their own legal costs and £9,000 cost contribution to the other side, the net benefit will be £45,999.

On this analysis, the probabilities expressed mathematically can be summarised as follows:

- Now

  The clients can receive a net £60,000 taking into account present own costs of £5,000.

- After trial

  There is a 25% probability of the clients losing and being £40,000 out of pocket and still owing the whole of the debt; there is a 37% probability of the client winning and receiving £70,001; there is a 12% probability of the clients winning but recovering nothing after judgment and still having to pay your legal costs of £25,000; there is a 26% probability of the clients winning the case but experiencing cost penalties that give them a net £45,999.

Thus described, most clients would instruct you to encourage a higher settlement figure now and then to settle.

A few words of caution are warranted for this approach. First, it must be remembered that the allocation of risk in the form of probabilities was intuitive, not scientific. The client also needs to take into account the background to the transaction when it is a single suit and not a dispute that is normal for the client's business (such as an insurance claim). In the case of the clients in 'A roof over their heads', only a judgment of the full amount might keep them from bankruptcy. They might, therefore, take the all or nothing approach.

Where clients are professional litigators, it might be possible to give a more mathematical account of the probabilities of win and loss based on actual like cases and the decisions made in the past. Since litigation and legal costs, and the risks inherent in them, are all part of the client's business, it is more likely that this technique would be applicable in almost every case.

7.7.3   Visual decision analysis

Decision analysis can be facilitated by working out a series of questions that the client should answer in order to come to a decision. They should be structured so that each question is in an appropriate sequence and so that each answer accumulates with previous answers. The sequence of questions should present a limited number of answers, usually no more than three. It is often in YES/NO form. This is usually far from easy. It forces the lawyer to re-examine his or her own analysis of the facts and legal issues in a rigorous way.

The decision analysis in question form quickly leads to chains of questions moving off in different directions. The presentation is made more comprehensible if the questions are set out in the form of an algorithm or a decision tree.

If it is the sort of case for which a mathematical probability analysis is possible, the mathematics can also be factored in. Here is such an analysis presented visually for the case of 'A roof over their heads' (see figure 7.3).

Figure 7.3

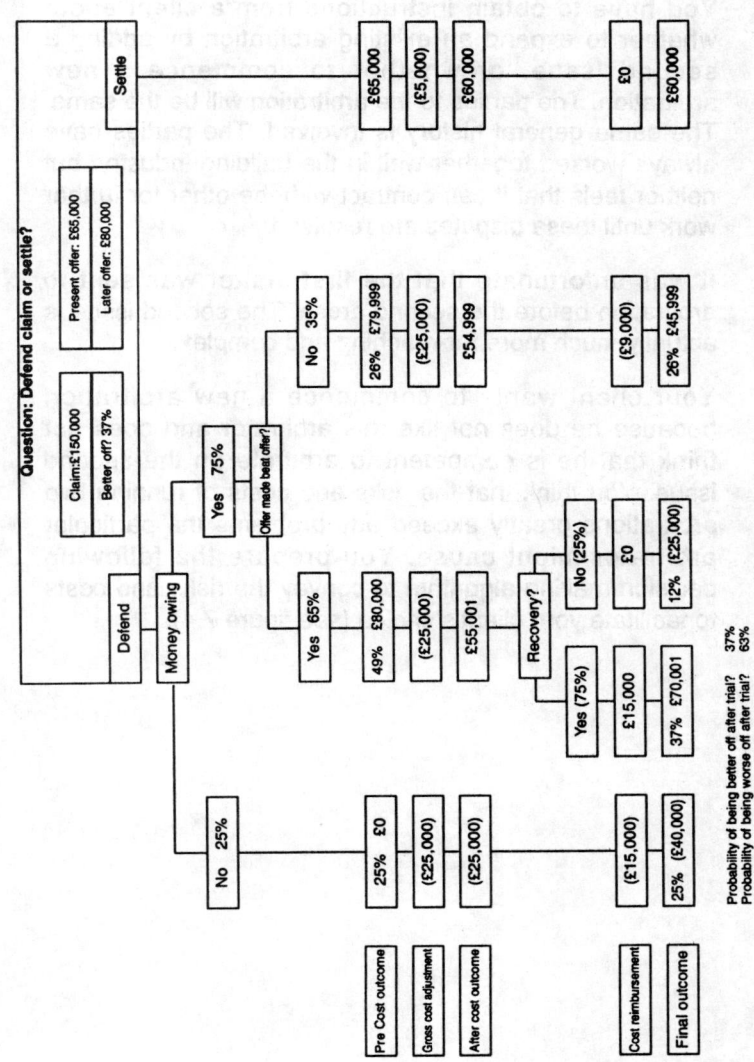

Case 7(D)

You have to obtain instructions from a client about whether to expand an existing arbitration by adding a second issue, or whether to commence a new arbitration. The parties to the arbitration will be the same. The same general history is involved. The parties have always worked together well in the building industry, but neither feels that it can contract with the other for further work until these disputes are resolved.

It was unfortunate that the first matter was sent to arbitration before the second arose. The second issue is actually much more far-reaching and complex.

Your client wants to commence a new arbitration because he does not like this arbitrator and does not think that he is competent to arbitrate on the second issue. You think that the risks and costs of running two arbitrations greatly exceed any problems the particular arbitrator might cause. You prepare the following decision-making algorithm to convey the risks and costs to facilitate your client's choice (see figure 7.4).

Solution Analysis 179

Figure 7.4

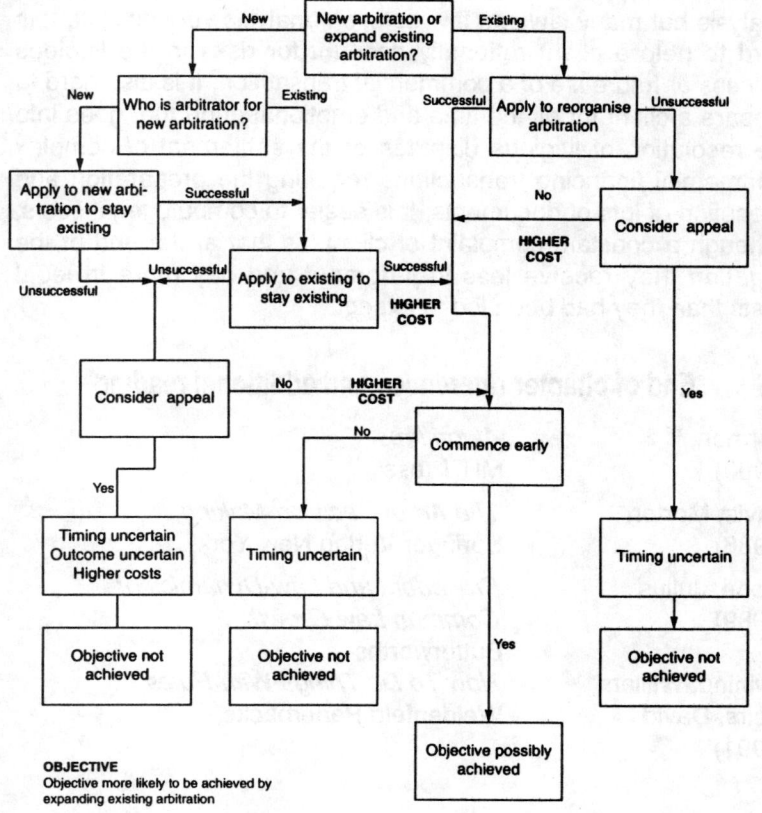

The representation of decisions in the form of decision trees or algorithms are subject to detailed rules. For decision trees see Davis (1986). For use of algorithms in law see Twining and Meirs (1991) and Cormen (1990). They force contractionary modes of thinking because they reveal, better than text, gaps, omissions or contradictions in reasoning.

7.8   Summary of solution analysis

Solution analysis is a shorter process to explain than problem analysis but many lawyers find solution analysis very difficult. It is hard to help a client rationally account for risks in the litigious process or future life of a commercial transaction. It is also hard to prepare a client for all the time and emotional effort that goes into the resolution of litigious disputes or the settlement of complex commercial financing transactions requiring the preparation and execution of lots of documents. It is easier to compute legal costs, although a constant complaint of clients is that at the end of the litigation they receive less in judgment and pay more in legal costs than they had been led to expect.

7.9   End of chapter references and additional reading

Cormen, T (1990)	*Algorithms* MIT Press	
Davis, Morton (1986)	*The Art of Decision-Making* Springer Verlag New York	
Stone, Julius (1989)	*Precedent and Law-Dynamics of Common Law Growth* Butterworths	
Twining, William Meirs, David (1991)	*How To Do Things With Rules* Weidenfeld Paperbacks	

CHAPTER

8 Implementation Analysis

'Talk does not cook rice.'

Chinese Proverb

**The Lawyer as
Co-ordinator**

8.1   The lawyer as co-ordinator with hat and shoes

Kolb describes the actor in the implementation phase as that of co-ordinator. When a lawyer implements a solution, he or she must co-ordinate the roles of the client (or various players if a corporate client), his or her own staff (word processor operators, secretaries, personal assistants, accounts department staff, photocopying, binding, database designers, desktop publishing staff), as well as people from the courts and other government bodies.

Implementation requires the donning of the white hat for facts and figures, and the black hat for what might be wrong. Where you only need follow set legal routines, you will be wearing either the formal navy shoes or the practical brown brogues. Sometimes you will need the orange gumboots for that urgent solution. In higher courts, lawyers don the ritualistic purple riding boots. (It is the client who winces at the strut.)

8.1.1 Implementation as talk or action

The implementation analysis phase is almost entirely about Action issues. True, you will need to check for changes in fact, law and client expectation as a Threshold issue if some time has elapsed since the last time you looked at the problem. In some cases, even at this late stage, a different view of the Fact or Law issues might emerge to return you to earlier stages in the problem solving process. For the most part, however, in the implementation phase you will read law for guidance about the steps that your client should now take.

In legal work, the Chinese proverb that talk does not cook rice is wrong. A clear explanation or a persuasive argument might be the only actions that count. This is probably more likely to be the case for matters involving the resolution of disputes (often involving minimising risk), than for commercial deals (often involving maximising profit).

But even commercial matters will involve an element of talk. Where parties are looking to maximise profit, any unnecessary delay or duplication of work in the implementation phase will have a more obvious influence on profit than possibilities overlooked or wrongly dismissed at the phases of situation appraisal, problem analysis or solution analysis.

Case 8(A)

> Your client is a major construction company that has retained you to do all the legal work in connection with finance for a project, making agreements with architects, quantity surveyors and sub-contractors and to be responsible for the leasing of all 51 storeys. Market conditions will largely determine what your client pays for land, fees and sub-contractors, and what your client receives in the letting.

In these circumstances, your 'talk' might make a major contribution to the matter. You might be able to negotiate favourably with government for tax concessions of one sort or another if the project is seen to be important to the community. Or you might dramatically rescue a looming industrial relations disaster by skilled and persuasive negotiation with the subcontractors. It is more likely, though, that the client would deal with these activities him or herself. The bulk of the work for the lawyer will be in developing systems that deliver a highly expert advice service with prompt advice and turn around of documents.

8.2   The continuum of talk

There are different kinds of talk that clinch the deal, some written, some spoken. They can be arranged along a kind of continuum, where the left represents the most objective version possible and the right represents argument unashamedly partisan.

Inform ⟶ Persuade ⟶ Negotiate ⟶ Advocate

In the case of 'A roof over their heads', one of the options was the solution to issue proceedings to recover money paid to the promoter under a scheme that actually required a prospectus. This sort of contentious dispute actually involves several implementation strategies running in tandem: first, a formal court proceeding where the action leading up to the trial is prescribed; second, a continuing dialogue with the other side and the client where the only limits on action are professional ethics and the deadlines set by the court procedure; third, arguments based on evidence and law that will be presented to the court on the day of the trial where the content of the argument varies with the skill and imagination of the advocate.

Many of the choices about implementation in this matter will be choices about what to say or what to write.

8.2.1   Tools for talk

Information

Information will try to present facts or rules in a way that all parties would assess to be correct. Even disputed facts can be presented as information in the sense that the version offered is clearly supported by the evidence, the only dispute being about whose version is believed.

Information will have the following qualities: completeness, correctness, clarity, coherence and comprehensibility. Information will use the following communication tools: plain language, diagrams, maps, flow charts, a visit to the site (often called a view).

Persuasion

Persuasion will sharpen the focus on one of perhaps several possible versions aiming to draw the listener into your version of the facts, or to make the inferences based on fact or fact and law that your argument needs. A persuasive case is one that is bespoke for the particular listener. It plays to the values, motivations, concerns and habitual language of the particular listener.

Persuasion will have the following qualities: omission of some information, emphasis of other information, implication as well as express statement. Persuasion uses the following tools: rhetorical devices such as overstatement, understatement, analogy, metaphor and careful selection of vocabulary. Persuasion often uses demonstrative evidence such as photographs or video reconstructions. Persuasion might make some fallacious arguments that are logically not valid but that appeal to the prejudice of the decision maker.

Negotiation

Negotiation involves the trading of information to reach a mutually acceptable solution. Negotiation is more structured than persuasion but less structured and partisan than advocacy. A negotiation that takes the form of a mutual problem solving activity might find the solicitor for one party proposing a solution for the other party that was even better than any posed by that party's own solicitor. It will be in the client's interest for the lawyer to be an even better lawyer for the other side, so long as one's own client benefits, too.

Negotiation should have the qualities of a mutually beneficial problem solving activity or at least a civilised decision to agree to disagree. Negotiation might use all or some of the tools of information and persuasion except that sometimes the lawyer will have to work harder to persuade his or her own client than the other lawyer.

Advocacy

Advocacy in this context is the role played by the advocate in the partisan court system where the advocate is only required to argue on behalf of a designated party or designated parties. Advocacy in this context is part information, part persuasion. As information it imposes its own constraints because advocates have certain obligations to the court, such as the obligation to reveal authorities that are against their own client's case. As persuasion, advocacy is also specialist. Persuasive advocates formulate the judgment that they wish the court to deliver, and then proceed to persuade the court why their version of events should be favoured.

Advocacy displays the following qualities: ability to formulate one's own argument as simply as possible, ability to anticipate arguments of the other side and to illustrate why each argument is weak or fallacious, and the ability to illustrate one's own argument by reference to similar fact situations likely to fall to the court for consideration. Advocates will use all the tools of information and persuasion, but will select the form that best represents the relevant content and chosen emphasis.

8.2.2   Information: the right talk and a further checklist

When trying to present the law or facts expressly and objectively, succinct statements and clear relationships will be important.

Figure 6.1 sets out a checklist for use at the problem analysis stage to help you understand the relationships between the law, the facts and the likely evidence or, in the case of a commercial transaction, the client's objectives.

Figure 8.1 sets out a checklist that will help you express the relationships between law and law and fact and law by using right words. You will see that you can use words to add (or co-ordinate) ideas when you are in expansionary thinking mode. You can also choose words to pattern ideas (or subordinate) when you are in contractionary thinking mode.

8.2.3   Persuasion: the right talk

Persuasion is dependent upon a familiarity with the person to be persuaded. You need to choose the right words and to conjure up the right experiences or the right images to persuade the particular listener.

When Lord Denning delivered judgment in *Miller v Jackson* [1977] QB 966 he chose his words for an audience of cricket lovers creating the elegiac picture of long summer afternoons:

> '... In the village of Lintz in County Durham they have their own ground, where they have played for these last 70 years. They tend it well. The wicket area is well rolled and mown. The outfield is kept short. It has a good club house for the players and seats for the onlookers ...'

Another commentator has described the same cricket ground quite differently:

> '... a scungy little ground surrounded by the worst artefacts of modern British industrialism ...'

Priestley (1990)

The second description might actually be more factual, but the first is no doubt better suited to Lord Denning's purpose in persuasion.

Highly abstract words often allow more people to agree with you. They include more concepts, for example, the concept of property encompasses all kinds of interest from fee simple in land to a mere equity. They allow for the listener to place their own interpretation, for example, the concept of freedom or motherhood. When needing to persuade a diverse audience, highly abstract words can allow you to gain agreement on points of principle.

8.2.4   An exercise in persuasion

Persuasion also depends upon the personality preference of the listener (see Chapter 2). Two examples will suffice for recall.

Figure 8.1

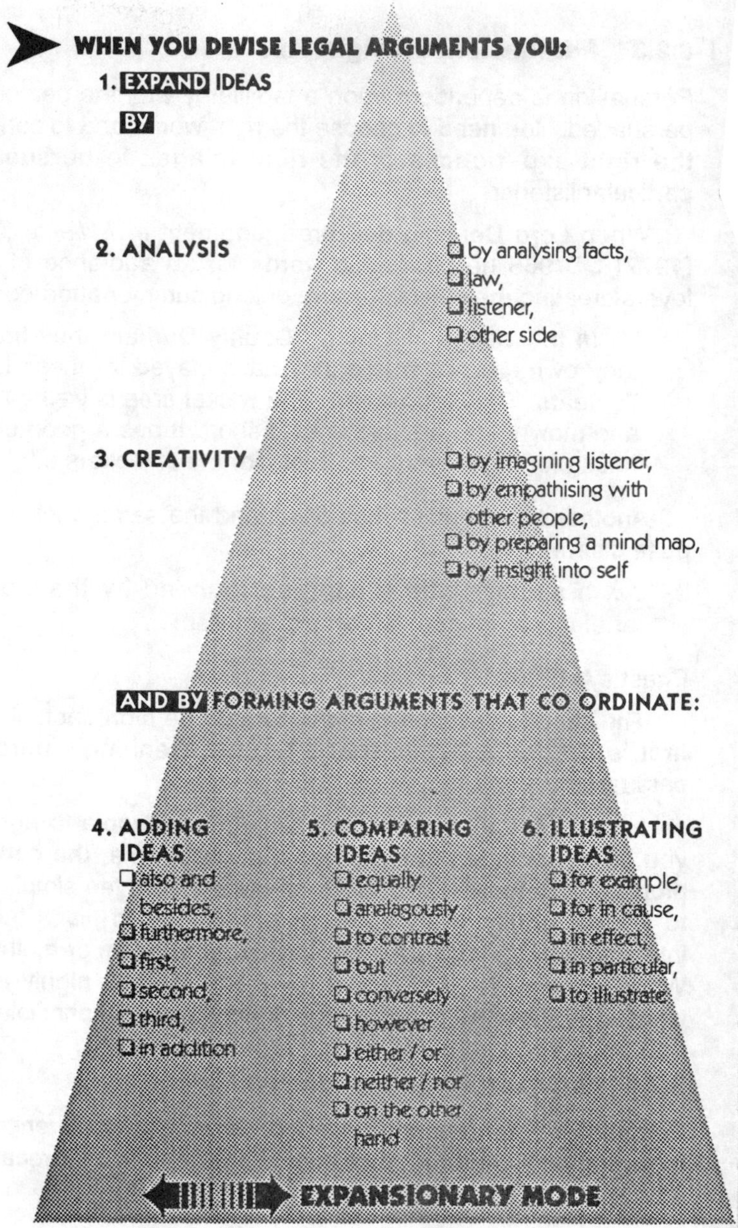

> **WHEN YOU DEVISE LEGAL ARGUMENTS YOU:**
> 1. **EXPAND** IDEAS
>   **BY**

2. ANALYSIS
- ❏ by analysing facts,
- ❏ law,
- ❏ listener,
- ❏ other side

3. CREATIVITY
- ❏ by imagining listener,
- ❏ by empathising with other people,
- ❏ by preparing a mind map,
- ❏ by insight into self

AND BY FORMING ARGUMENTS THAT CO ORDINATE:

4. ADDING IDEAS
- ❏ also and besides,
- ❏ furthermore,
- ❏ first,
- ❏ second,
- ❏ third,
- ❏ in addition

5. COMPARING IDEAS
- ❏ equally
- ❏ analagously
- ❏ to contrast
- ❏ but
- ❏ conversely
- ❏ however
- ❏ either / or
- ❏ neither / nor
- ❏ on the other hand

6. ILLUSTRATING IDEAS
- ❏ for example,
- ❏ for in cause,
- ❏ in effect,
- ❏ in particular,
- ❏ to illustrate

◀║║║║║▶ **EXPANSIONARY MODE**

AND YOU:

6. CONTRACT IDEAS BY SUBORDINATION
   BECAUSE OF

7. CAUSE AND EFFECT
- ❑ and so,
- ❑ accordingly,
- ❑ as a result,
- ❑ because,
- ❑ consequently,
- ❑ therefore,
- ❑ thus

8. OTHER TIME RELATIONSHIPS
- ❑ before,
- ❑ after,
- ❑ at the same time,
- ❑ during,
- ❑ now,
- ❑ once,
- ❑ formerly,
- ❑ until,
- ❑ when

9. CONDITIONS SET OUT
- ❑ as though,
- ❑ even though,
- ❑ granted that,
- ❑ if,
- ❑ unless,
- ❑ provided,
- ❑ on condition that,
- ❑ as a condition precedent,
- ❑ as a condition subsequent

10. CONCLUSIONS DRAWN
- ❑ in short,
- ❑ in summary,
- ❑ in conclusion,
- ❑ above all,
- ❑ after all,
- ❑ unquestionably

 **CONTRACTIONARY MODE**

A listener who takes a rule and fact based approach will be more persuaded by a clear exposition of the facts, the law and how they inexorably lead to your proposed conclusion. Such listeners often determine relevance narrowly and are more persuaded by an argument delivered in the order of importance they have determined, giving emphasis to arguments that they consider of greatest importance and complexity and focusing on the facts at hand. Precision in the use of language will be important and where there is a choice, use the most concrete language possible.

On the other hand, in the same case, a listener who takes a big picture approach might be happy to explore all possibilities in less detail and will be more concerned about how this decision fits into the law generally as well as the validity or fairness of the instant decision to be made. Such a person will allow you to use more abstract language.

At its most rhetorical, persuasion works because you choose the right word to fit the expectations of the listener. The right word will rarely be a neutral description or definition. The right word will be coloured by the views of the listener.

This technique is used in journalism all the time. Let us imagine, for example, that you are preparing an article on particular professions and that you need to find pithy collective nouns that encapsulate not only what the profession does, but also how their clients might feel about certain behaviour.

The clients of architects that you have consulted were unanimous in telling you that the architect seemed to listen to what they wanted but presented a design that did not resemble the clients' description. The most appropriate descriptive noun for architects in this context might be an *anarchy* of architects.

Try to find a persuasive collective noun for each of the following professions, taking into account the audience perspective:

- a group of police constables, when addressing an audience of experienced student activists;

- a group of accountants, when addressing an audience of inventors who hate being told about the capital needed to launch their product;

- a group of psychiatrists, when addressing a medical audience deeply sceptical about that speciality;

- a group of barristers, when addressing an audience of clients.

Tim Lindsey has illustrated his response to my suggestions at figure 8.2. If you find the pictures funny, but the phrases puzzling, perhaps you could prepare similar expressions that would persuade you.

Figure 8.2 (1)

A Crunch of Constable

Figure 8.2 (2)

An Awful of Accountants

Figure 8.2 (3)

A Psilly of Psychiatrists

Figure 8.2 (4)

A Boast of Barristers

8.3   Implementation as action

Writing a letter, interviewing a witness, or negotiating with the other side are actions available to a lawyer that might solve the client's problem and that involve talk.

Other skills of implementation are coming to the fore, for example, knowledge of other industries and non-legal ways of doing things; the ability to use computer technology to process data in large volumes; the ability to harness the skills of a diverse team so that they do not work at cross-purposes; the ability to design a system of documents rather than merely to draft a single document. The failures of implementation will be failures of leading, planning, motivating and controlling.

8.3.1   Action: a procedural or a strategic approach

Why do we do some things as lawyers? The answer is sometimes because they have always been done that way. Those ways might be good but other ways might be better. Often lawyers are selling essentially the same solutions. The only way that you will be able to distinguish yourself from competitor lawyers is by how you implement the solution, not by what the solutions achieves. Solutions that are faster, cheaper or more efficient will be just as much in demand as solutions that are better. From the client's perspective implementation of a legal problem sometimes creates a bigger problem that the problem the implementation seeks to solve.

A strategic approach to the implementation of any legal solution will first analyse the goals the client seeks to achieve, counsel the client on what can realistically be achieved and will then map out a series of steps with a timetable to achieve those goals. A strategic approach drives the matter to conclusion in minimum time, recognising for most people that time is money.

8.3.2   Expansionary and contractionary modes

When thinking about implementation, you will add possible ways of implementing the solution to the list. When you think the list is complete, it is often useful to try a couple of expansionary modes of thinking. The expansionary modes of thinking dealt with below are:

- the 'do little' activity;
- the 'how they did it in other files' activity;
- standing in the shoes of the other side;
- new machines, new ways.

In selecting modes of implementation, you will eliminate possible ways and prioritise those left. You will be using contractionary modes of thinking. When you think that you have completed the selection process, it is useful to try out some contractionary modes of thinking that are particularly appropriate for this stage. The contractionary modes of thinking dealt with below are:

- climate change checklist;
- fallacies in argument;
- the checklist;
- action as project management;
- the Murphy's law analysis.

A checklist summarising this process is contained at figure 8.3.

8.4   Expansionary tools for implementation analysis

Although it is not always possible to add further solutions to those already suggested by reasoning through the Law issues or those that might be suggested by the client, it is usually possible to devise different ways of implementing the same solution.

8.4.1   The 'do little' solution

It is always worth asking the heinous question before acting: what would happen if the client did nothing, or did nothing for a time?

Sometimes, a client comes to you afire for action out of understandable irritation and frustration. The time and effort involved in working through the problem as a legal solution has a therapeutic effect and the solutions so desired from the lawyer at the outset become less desirable as time rolls on and costs mount. The vengeful divorce or the acid arbitration are good examples of this.

8.4.2   The 'how they did it in other files' solution

You should always check with other lawyers in your firm or in other firms, where you have a matter that is new to you, that what you propose to do is what would normally be done by lawyers in a similar circumstance. This is a practical way of avoiding claims in professional negligence where the standard is based on what other lawyers would do. More practically, it might save your client a lot of money and time.

8.4.3   Standing in the shoes of the other side

You can adjust your solution by remembering at this stage to focus on the expectations of the other side in litigious transactions. If you know as much about their client and their case as they do, you might be able to suggest a solution that is more valuable for their client, but costs your client less.

One creative example springs to mind. The client (the defendant in this case) was the insurer of an accountant who had

Figure 8.3

THE LAWYER AS CO-ORDINATOR — A CHECKLIST FOR

WHEN YOU IMPLEMENT THE CLIENT'S PREFERRED SOLUTION YOU:

1. **EXPAND** THE POSSIBLE TECHNIQUES FOR USE IN IMPLEMENTATION

   BY

2. CHECKING
   - other files,
   - other lawyers files,
   - other firm's techniques

3. SEEKING ANALOGIES — in other professions

4. SEEKING EFFICIENCIES — in machine, in job design

5. ANTICIPATING WHAT WILL BE DONE OR REQUIRED BY THE OTHER SIDE

6. REMEMBERING TO KEEP PLAN 'B' IN MIND

7. **TO FORM** A FINAL PLAN

⟷ EXPANSIONARY MODE

© Margot Costanzo 1994

IMPLEMENTATION ANALYSIS

▶ **AND YOU:**

8. **CONTRACT** AND FOCUS THE FINAL PLAN INTO ACTION.

   BY

9. **LISTING TASKS**

10. **PREPARING BUDGETS**
    - ❑ time
    - ❑ cost

11. **MARSHALLING TEAM**
    - ❑ allocating roles
    - ❑ allocating tasks

12. **SPECIFYING DEADLINES ESPECIALLY FOR CRITICAL STEPS**

13. **MARSHALLING EQUIPMENT**

14. **USING VISUAL REPRESENTATION TO CONTROL**
    - ❑ a whiteboard
    - ❑ checklist
    - ❑ flowcharts
    - ❑ GANT charts
    - ❑ pert (CPM charts)
    - ❑ algorithms

15. **UPDATING FOR CHANGE AND MANAGING SETBACKS**

16a. **REPORTING TO CLIENT FOR REVISED INSTRUCTIONS**

16b. **GOING BACK TO SITUATION APPRAISAL FOR MAJOR PROBLEMS NOT ANTICIPATED**

17. **REPORTING TO TEAM**

18. **SUMMARISING RESULTS ON COMPLETION**
    - ❑ to client – including billing and collection
    - ❑ to team to enable comparison between how you thought the matter would go and how it actually went
    - ❑ the firm, if procedures need revising

||||▶ ◀|||| **CONTRACTIONARY MODE**

been sued for preparing an allegedly negligent financial report about a company the plaintiff was thinking of buying. The accountant was well meaning but simply not competent to hand this complex analysis. At the time the action arose, indemnity insurance was not compulsory for accountants and most accountants had coverage of less than £100,000. This particular accountant had coverage of more than double that amount. His assets were limited to a modest house and his share of a not very profitable accountancy practice. The amount for which the accountant was insured was not obliged to be disclosed to the plaintiff in this jurisdiction.

During the settlement negotiations, the solicitor for the plaintiff revealed his assumption that the accountant had few assets and that his coverage was likely to be less than £100,000. The solicitor for the defendant indemnity insurer neither confirmed nor denied that observation. He then made an offer to the plaintiff's solicitor that would give the appearance of confirming that belief. The plaintiff accepted the offer.

This strategy for implementation had been devised by the defendant and his solicitor from the outset of the transaction in anticipation that this, like most of these disputes, would settle. They had gone to some trouble to research the historical insurance position of accountants at that time in order to be able to see the case from the plaintiff's solicitor's perspective.

A good negotiator will also be alive to the possibility that different people value the same things in different ways. This gives each client the possibility of feeling that they have won even on the same settlement terms.

8.4.4   New machines, new ways

Many lawyers still practise as though the only benefits conferred on them by science were the development of movable type by Gutenberg in the 16th century and the development of photocopying in the 20th century. They use word processors with powerful capabilities as though they were just memory typewriters. Phones that can store numbers, that can be diverted to a third location or be hooked into a computer system for automatic costing or that can receive voicemail messages, are only used to make and receive calls.

New machines can give you new ways to provide greater efficiency and access to clients. Many law firms now provide documents to clients on line for checking and for giving instructions.

New machines and increased literacy also mean that some clients are pressing for completely new ways of doing legal work. Banks and building societies are increasingly bringing all their standard financing documentation in-house. The role of the external lawyer becomes that of designing the suite of documents that the client will need for most standard transactions and of teaching the client's staff how to complete them, often under the supervision of the in-house lawyer. In some debt collection practices, a major client might have access to the lawyer's database so that it can look up a status report on the collection of debts for itself.

New machines bring a need for new knowledge and much greater skill in managing and co-ordinating the contribution of each new machine and its operator. The wondrous machines that can accomplish the impossible still take some time. For example, the inability to predict how long photocopying documents actually takes is still a potent source of embarrassment in court. I have seen experienced lawyers rush back to the office to have 200 pages copied from various bound volumes over lunchtime, only to have the office manager patiently explain that bound volumes need to be hand copied and will take more time. It is then up to the lawyer to rush back to court and explain to the judge (who often has an even slighter understanding of the practicalities of the technology than that possessed by the lawyer) that the promise made before lunch cannot be fulfilled after lunch.

As more lawyers themselves operate this equipment, the capacity to take into account the time that things actually take will improve.

8.5   Contractionary tools for implementation analysis

8.5.1   Climate change checklist

As usual, if some time has elapsed since you last looked at the file, check that nothing material in the climate, the facts or the law has changed so that the conditions and assumptions under which you are acting still apply.

8.5.2   Fallacies in argument

When the implementation involves talk in the form of an argument made by you or someone else, it is always worthwhile examining your argument for some of the fallacies in logic that abound in popular culture. Philosophers have specialist names for these fallacies, but I have focused on issues of relevance and on assumptions only.

Circularity

When the Birmingham Six attempted to commence a civil action against the police, Lord Denning said:

> 'Just consider the course of events if this action is allowed to proceed to trial. If the six men fail it will mean much time and money has been expended for no good purpose. If the six men win it will mean that the police are guilty of perjury, that they are guilty of violence and threats, that the confessions were invented and improperly admitted in evidence and the convictions were erroneous. That would mean that the Home Secretary would have to recommend they should be pardoned or remit the case to the Court of Appeal. This is such an appalling vista that every sensible person in the land would say it cannot be right that these actions should go further. This case shows what a civilised country we are. The State has lavished large sums of money in their defence. On their own evidence they are

guilty. It is high time it stopped because this is really an attempt to set aside their convictions. It is a scandal which should not be allowed to continue.'

Quoted from Kennedy (1992)

The assertion that if the application fails, time and money would have been spent to no good purpose is a judgment only the applicants are qualified to make. It is also a judgment that might be made about at least one side in all litigious applications, since one side is bound to lose. It is an irrelevant judgment.

The projected implications of the six winning are described as appalling, but it is for the judge to decide according to the law, irrespective of a value judgment about the consequences. In fact, the argument fails to take this spectre to its truly logical conclusion, namely if the case needs overturning and their pardon is justified, it is the injustice against the six that is truly appalling. The means of overturning the injustice would be praiseworthy, not appalling.

The money expended on their defence, and indeed the issue of whether the State can be said to be civilised on that basis or any other is also irrelevant to the application.

The assertion that the six are guilty on their own evidence is a naughty piece of circularity. Presumably, Lord Denning was referring to the confessions. If the confessions were not properly obtained, they should have been inadmissible. Perhaps the confessions were a vital piece of evidence without which there would have been no guilty verdict at all.

Lord Denning shows a general circularity in argument. It is not for a judge on such an application to decide because of the consequences flowing from a decision. It is for him to make the decision based on the law and for others to deal with the consequences.

Other fallacies found in legal argument are as follows.

Arguing from ignorance

We argue from ignorance when we say that if we do not know a particular conclusion to be true we conclude it is false. Or, if we cannot prove that a statement is false we accept that it is true. Only if we look for evidence and cannot find what should be there can we draw a conclusion either way.

False alternatives

These are most commonly presented as the all or nothing option. When the argument represents fewer alternatives to choose from than the number of alternatives that actually exist then the alternatives are described as false. Politicians use this fallacy all the time, 'you are either with me or you are against me'.

Straw man

This term is used when someone puts up an argument superficially similar to yours and then defends it with a conclusion good for that person but bad for you. For example, if the other side summarises your argument in law by citing weaker statements from a judgment than you would cite and then drawing favourable conclusions, this might be a fallacious argument if you cite stronger statements that do not lead to your opponent's conclusion.

Attacking the person

An argument that is attacked due to factors about the person who makes it, rather than on its own merits is also a fallacious argument. In some societies, uncorroborated evidence is impeached if given by a woman. The character of the complainant, revealed in prior sexual history, in a sexual assault case could be seen as this kind of fallacy. A sexually active person is neither more or less credible than one who is not. Evidence that a person consented to sexual activity in the past with other people is not evidence that the person consented on this occasion.

8.5.3   The checklist

A checklist is a chronological list of all the things that need to be checked or done. They can be complex, for example, as in the checklist completed by an airline pilot before each takeoff. Checklists are particularly useful when lots of items must be completed routinely in circumstances where the problem solver is likely to lose concentration because of volume or to be bored by repetition. Lawyers use checklists in all kinds of ways. As a reminder for information to be obtained from a client at the time instructions are taken; as a control tool to ensure that all documents have been received within given time limits and from diverse sources; as a way of allocating different tasks in one transaction to different people so that everyone knows what everyone else should be doing and when.

8.5.4   Action as project management

The construction industry has developed very sophisticated tools to help decide what should be done by whom and when in a construction project. Many of these are now available as computer software packages, such as Microsoft Project.

Project management takes a strategic approach by creating visual tools to give the co-ordinators of a project an overview of the whole project with budgets both for time and for money.

The essence of project management is the ability to:

- list all the basic tasks required to complete the transaction;
- identify tasks that are critical to the completion of the project and deadlines for the completion of those critical tasks;
- assess three time estimates for completion of all tasks, especially critical tasks – the most probable time, the most optimistic time and the most pessimistic time;

- assess which tasks are dependent upon the completion of other tasks before they can be commenced;
- co-ordinate the input of all parties involved before the solution is embarked upon so that all relevant factors can be taken into account in this process;
- prepare a plan setting tasks, dates and allocating roles;
- revise the plan constantly as soon as something changes.

Project management uses two visual tools to present the original plan and to report progress – the GANT chart and the PERT/CPM chart.

A GANT chart is a time schedule for each person that visually represents how long each step is to take. If you are a co-ordinator of the project, you only need to look at the GANT chart to work out what someone should be working on at any point in the project.

A PERT/CPM chart sets out how tasks and time interrelate. Each task is represented by a box. Tasks that are dependent on each other are joined by lines. The sum total of the lines sets out the critical path of the project. The PERT/CPM chart enables anyone working on the project to see how their tasks relate to other tasks. If they are unable to meet their deadline they can inform those who are to be effected so that they might be able to deploy their time on other tasks rather than just hanging around.

Some lawyers use this project management system in its entirety. Some adapt it for use on smaller matters and with smaller groups of people.

The distinctive feature of this approach is that it is strategic, not procedural. You cannot just start on the first step of a procedure and assume that you will jump through other hoops from time to time. You need to plan what you will be doing, and how long it will take, and to carefully reassess the implications of change at any one step on all other steps.

Implementation as a managed project enables the co-ordinator to make informed decisions about whether, or how, the project might complete faster. Tasks that would traditionally have been performed by one lawyer serially might be performed by several lawyers simultaneously with no greater cost to the client.

A managed project also reduces the time spent on crisis management. By its very nature a managed project formalises planning as the first step in implementation. The only problems that then arise for separate consideration will be issues that require further client instructions or steps that go wrong in ways that the co-ordinator had not foreseen.

Techniques for project management are discussed fully in Baker (1992).

8.5.5   The Murphy's Law analysis

The only thing that can be said for certain in the implementation phase of any legal matter, like implementation in any other matter, is that something is bound to go wrong.

It helps to try and assess at the outcome of a transaction where and when the sticking points might occur. In legal transactions, as soon as you require the co-operation or agreement of any other person, including people in your own firm, be prepared for that to be a sticking point sometimes. Anything will take longer if you don't set a deadline and it often takes longer even if you do. Work requiring creative input has a more variable delivery factor than work that is analytical or mechanical.

You can only be criticised for something going wrong where it is something that you did not anticipate. Remember, in preparing your plan for implementation, you always have an alternative for something that goes wrong.

8.6   Summary of implementation

Implementation analysis requires fewer legal skills and more management skills than other phases of problem solving. With the advent of computers and the need to share data and resources, lawyers are becoming better at management of the client's matter. And so we should. We need to remember that failures in implementation can be just as fatal in terms of cost and delay to the client as advice that is wrong in law.

Transplant operations may be examples of acute medical problems for the patient, but they are examples of superb project management by the staff. The same could not be said for every acute client issue which comes to court or which enters a lawyer's office. Lawyers have focused most of their education on the thinking process that takes place in the mind. We need to continue to develop tools that enable this process to be represented on the page. Once problem solving has been recorded and systematised the processes themselves can be checked, changed, shortened, agreed upon, delegated, shared with other lawyers and those of other professions, redesigned and made simpler.

We name landmark principles after legal clients who pay for the case but perhaps we should be like physicians and name tools for analysing, solving and implementing legal solutions after their inventors.

Most of the questions that will arise after the implementation analysis will involve choices about what to do and many will be based on law issues that were researched in the problem analysis phase.

Whether you need to invoke this problem solving process again in any matter after you have embarked upon implementation will depend on the matter's complexity and on your capacity to anticipate and to plan. Every time you need to seek your client's instructions you might have a problem that needs to be run through these four phases, starting at situation appraisal. Certainly the scale of problems to be solved in the same matter often reduces even though the process of moving from thought to action remains the same. Occasionally, however, the problems that need to be solved through the process will just keep on growing. A piece of litigation for one client might end up being a class action for many. The innocuous legal problem to be resolved by one letter of advice might require many different documents and expert opinions.

Chapters 5-8 assume that you can follow this step by step process for each problem you are trying to solve. The checklists synthesise the information in each chapter at a high level of generality so that you can have a dialogue with yourself by looking at only one page rather than a whole chapter.

The final chapter in this book proposes a further synthesis of this four-phase process into a moving model. This model more closely approximates not only the mess from which you need to extract the problem to be solved but also the mess that the problem solving activity itself often becomes.

End of chapter references and additional reading

Baker, Sunny   *On Time, On Budget*
Baker, Kim   Prentice Hall
(1992)

Priestley LJ   '*The Writing of judgments: A forum*'
(1990)   Australian Bar Review p 140

CHAPTER

9 The Complete Problem Solver - A Further Model

'I liked your opera. I think I will set it to music.'

Ludwig van Beethoven

The great Australian Chief Justice Sir Owen Dixon is reputed to have preferred writing his own reasons, even when he concurred with brother judges. Lawyers have a habit of preferring their own words. It is to be anticipated that in a profession peopled by such determined individualists, not every lawyer will see the point in trying to construct a model for legal problem solving in words. Even those who can see the point of words might be alienated by pictures.

Sometimes the attempt to define and to describe the obvious can be helpful. Once it is expressed, the obvious can then be delegated, taught, critiqued and improved.

9.1 The model so far

We started with a wide definition of problem solving as something extracted from the 'mess' which is the general situation (Chapter One). We noted the mind's tricks in the process of perceiving visual and auditory facts in that 'mess' (Chapter Two). We noted the ways in which personality preference might affect conception of the problem by the lawyer (Chapter Three).

We have seen that clients have their own conceptions of what the law is to achieve. They will come to a lawyer either to resolve a contentious dispute or to set up business relationships for the future (Chapter One). Clients think about law in terms of action to be taken. Lawyers think about law in terms of legal issues to resolve. A client might come with only one problem to be solved, but the lawyer has many problems within this problem to resolve before the matter is finished. For example, the client's objective might be to have contracts exchanged by next week; however,

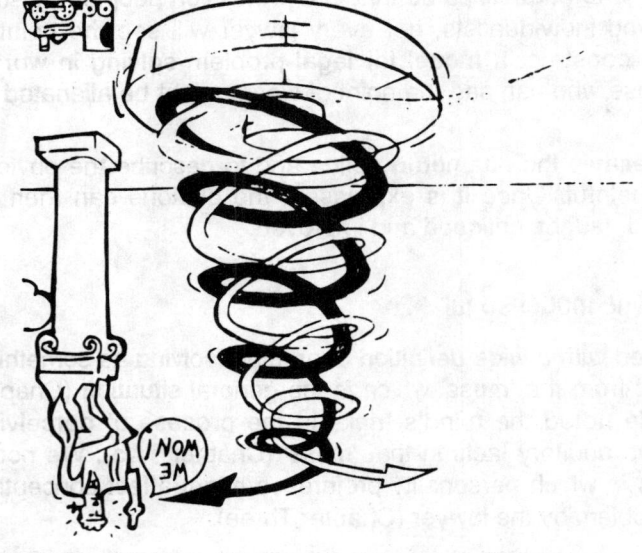

the lawyer might have to resolve many internal problems of drafting before this can be achieved.

The lawyer will therefore be dealing with four kinds of content: Threshold issues (personalities, ethics, firm constraints and change); Fact issues (determining belief, opinion, corroborative fact and evidence); Law issues (matching life words and law words, facts with evidence, relevant facts with law) and Action issues (deciding what to do and having reasons for this).

We noted earlier that some of the problems revealed by an analysis of complaints against lawyers are about a lack of system. If the problem solver was trying to make an effort to solve a problem systematically, particularly in a team where the need for a shared system is more obvious, he or she would need to follow a step by step system though time.

In analysing problem solving, we adapted Kolb's model of problem solving, noting that it has four stages:

- situation appraisal;
- problem analysis;
- solution analysis;
- implementation analysis.

If a lawyer were attempting to move to a systematic approach to problem solving either as an individual, or as a team effort, this model could be followed by beginning with situation analysis and proceeding through each stage. For each stage a list of questions was suggested in earlier chapters, which the lawyer should have processed by the end of each stage in relation to each of the four content areas: Threshold, Fact, Law and Action. These four broad stages could be internalised as a routine for use alone or in a group.

We noted that, at each of the four stages in the process, the thinker used both expansionary modes of thinking and contractionary modes of thinking.

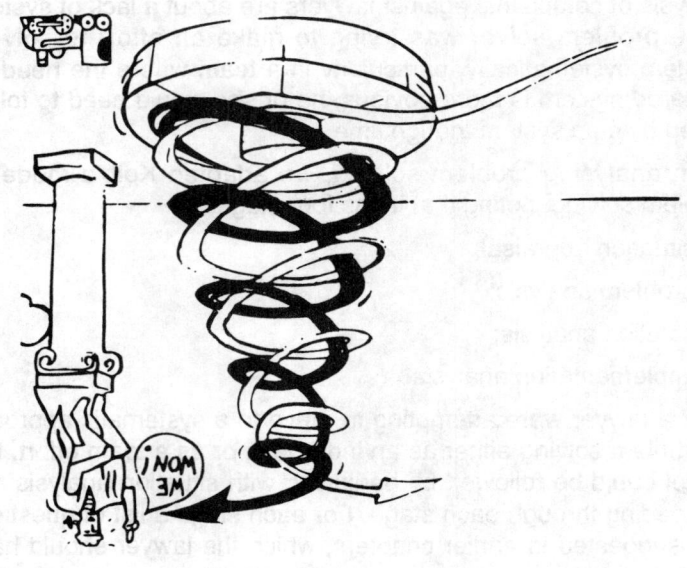

In expansionary modes of thinking, more matters to think about were added to the lists for Law issues and Action issues. In contractionary modes of thinking, items were deleted from both these lists so that the thinking could be focused and summarised and therefore taken into the next stage.

Sometimes the thinking in the contractionary stage would lead to the conclusion that the previous phase needed to be redone.

9.1.1 The model with checklists

The checklist of content, possible thinking techniques, useful rules of thumb, and things to avoid became quite long. Each phase was therefore summarised into a checklist.

A further checklist to help choose language at the stage of implementation analysis was added because of the special importance of language in law as expressing the meaning of each idea as well as the relationships between them.

The four checklists dealing with the four stages of problem solving (at Figures 5.3, 6.1, 7.2, 8.1 and 8.3) can be synthesised into a higher level of generality as a summary in overview. The summary has the benefit of being on one page. This summary is proposed as a substitute for the Kolb model and the various other models set out in Chapter 4 and is set out in figure 9.1.

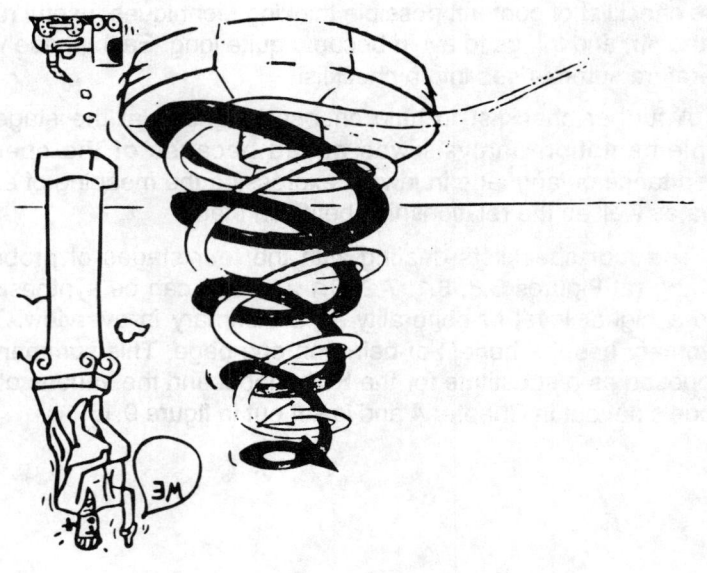

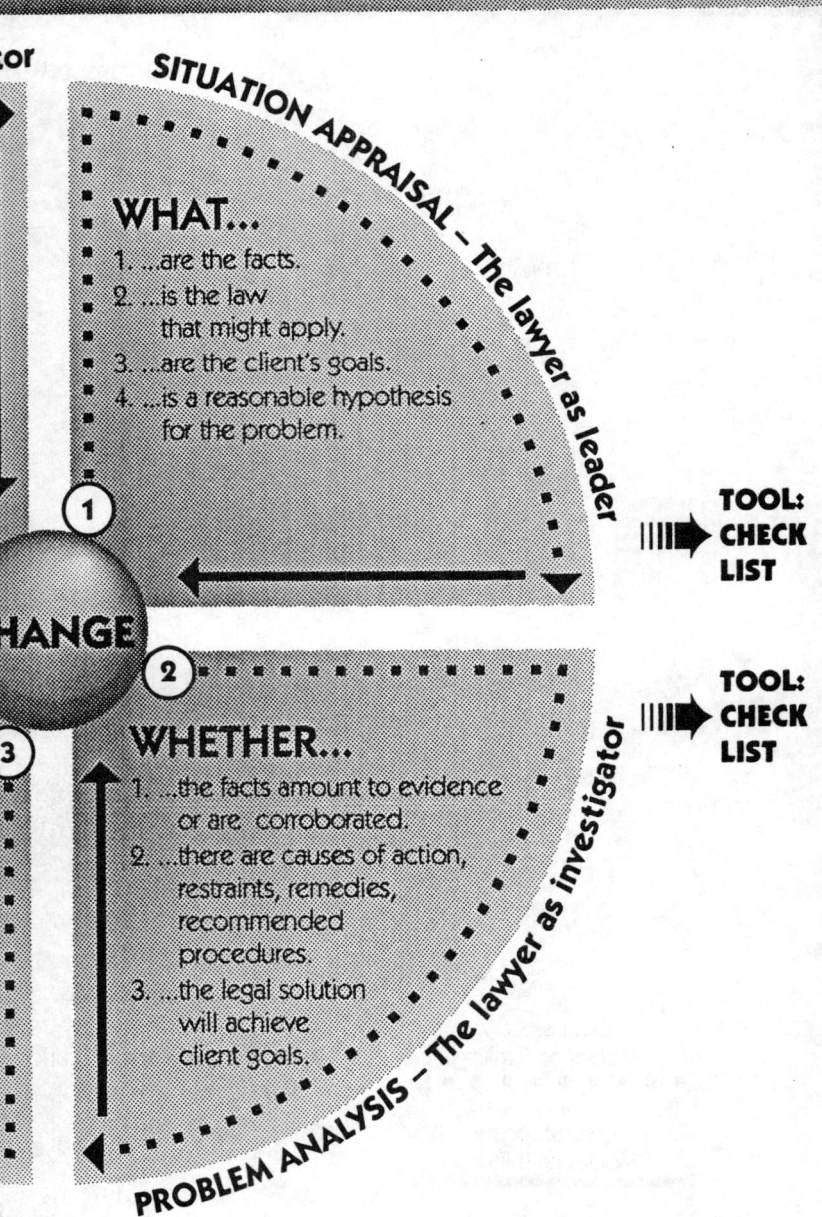

FOR LEGAL PROBLEM SOLVING

tor

SITUATION APPRAISAL – The lawyer as leader

WHAT...

1. ...are the facts.
2. ...is the law that might apply.
3. ...are the client's goals.
4. ...is a reasonable hypothesis for the problem.

1

HANGE

2

3

TOOL:
CHECK
LIST

TOOL:
CHECK
LIST

WHETHER...

1. ...the facts amount to evidence or are corroborated.
2. ...there are causes of action, restraints, remedies, recommended procedures.
3. ...the legal solution will achieve client goals.

PROBLEM ANALYSIS – The lawyer as investigator

Figure 9.1

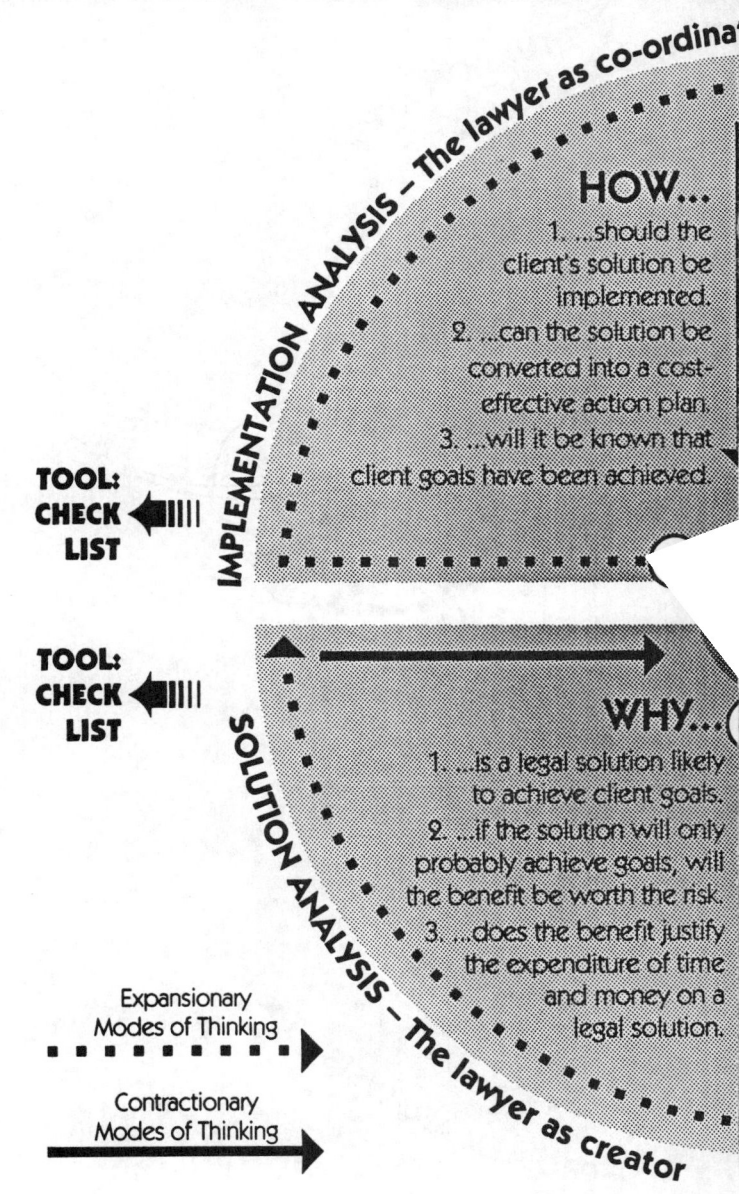

IMPLEMENTATION ANALYSIS – The lawyer as co-ordina'

HOW...
1. ...should the client's solution be implemented.
2. ...can the solution be converted into a cost-effective action plan.
3. ...will it be known that client goals have been achieved.

TOOL: CHECK LIST

TOOL: CHECK LIST

SOLUTION ANALYSIS – The lawyer as creator

WHY...
1. ...is a legal solution likely to achieve client goals.
2. ...if the solution will only probably achieve goals, will the benefit be worth the risk.
3. ...does the benefit justify the expenditure of time and money on a legal solution.

Expansionary Modes of Thinking

Contractionary Modes of Thinking

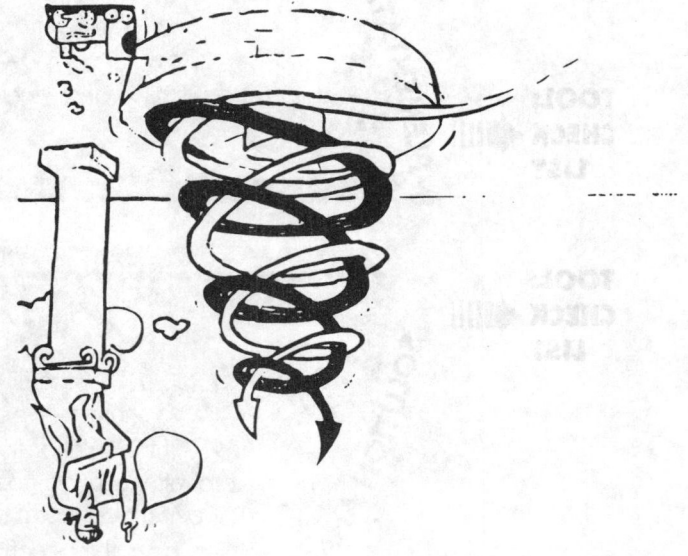

At this higher level of generality, the focus for each phase is concentrated into questions with a single focus.

Situation analysis

What

- are the facts?
- is the law that might apply?
- are the client's goals?
- is a reasonable hypothesis for this problem?

Problem analysis

Whether

- the facts amount to evidence or are corroborated;
- there are causes of action, restraint, remedies, recommended procedures;
- the legal solution will achieve client goals.

Solution analysis

Why

- is a legal solution likely to achieve client goals?
- if the solution is likely to achieve those goals, is the benefit worth the risk?
- does the benefit justify the expenditure of time and money on the solution?

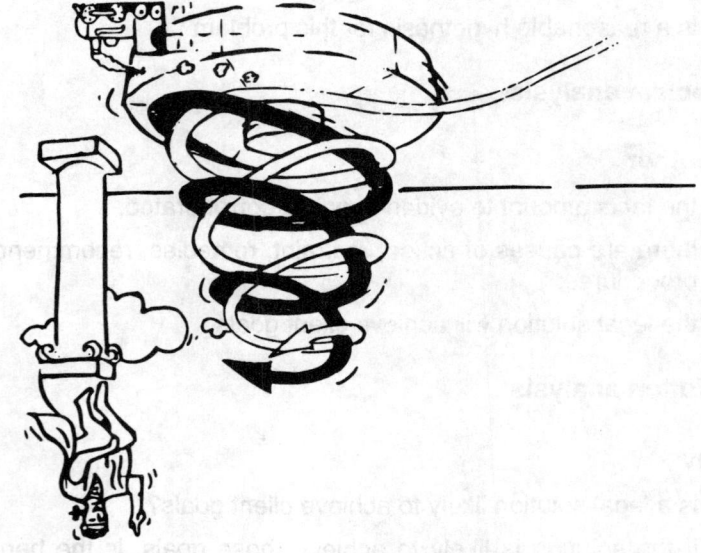

Implementation analysis

How

- should the solution be implemented?
- can the solution be converted into a cost-effective action plan?
- can the achievement (or not) of the client's goals be evaluated?

It is appropriate that the four stages of the problem solving process be represented in a circle. The reality of daily problem solving is that we often start the process at another stage than at situation analysis; for example, the client might come in with a specific idea about implementation. We hop from phase to phase in a random way until we can calibrate the dimensions of the problem and then start with situation analysis. In a circle, the content can start anywhere and can dart across the centre to any other place. The only requirement of the systematic process we have discussed that cannot be avoided is change.

Whenever another phase is entered, the problem solver must deal with change. A change in facts, law and expectation is another constant like the climate. Change is at the heart of all legal transactions, so I have placed it at the centre of the wheel.

Finally the content is turned around in the mind in either expansionary or the contractionary thinking mode. This is represented by arrows. The broken arrow represents expansionary thinking; the solid arrow represents contractionary thinking. Specific examples of thinking tools used in each mode at each stage are given in the checklists.

9.1.2 A textual model

The four checklists together with the summary overview add up to a complete textual model of problem solving at two levels of generality. The overview is a synthesis at a high level of

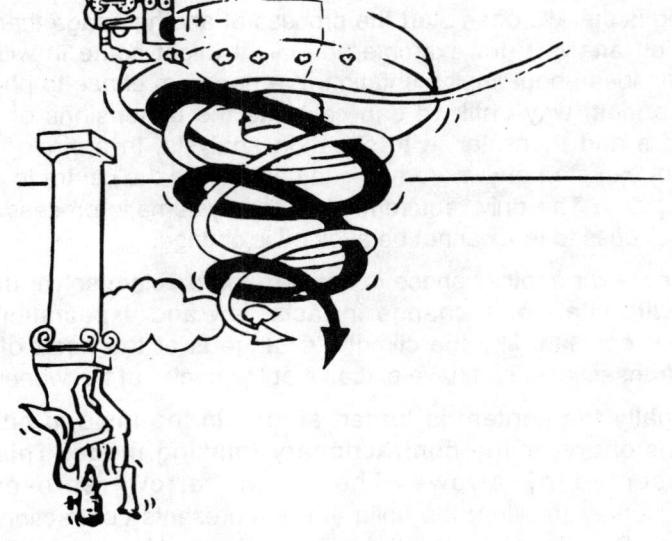

generality but still more detailed than the models given in Chapter 4, with a specifically legal focus, and some attempt has been made to set out the reasoning process in the spiralling or almost random process that real legal thinking sometimes resembles.

This is a model that will satisfy personality preferences for analysis and words. You might like to think of it as the equivalent of an IBM computer model, pre-Windows.

9.2 A model in words and pictures

The greatest limitation of the textual model is that it only lives in the mind, not on the page. A textual model can be coloured, but not animated. In the era of multi-media interactive virtual reality, it seems a shame to settle for something that could not adapted for use with all that marvellous technology. This kind of model would satisfy personality preferences for visual representation. What follows is a problem solving model in pictures.

The climate

Professions work in a specialist environment. They are constrained by the ethical considerations of their profession which amount to:

- whether they may act;
- whether they should act;
- how they may act.

These considerations can arise at any time during a legal transaction. You might discover at the outset that your firm or employer has a conflict of interest and so the whole organisation is restrained from acting for a client. Some way into the matter, specialist advice might be needed, requiring the involvement of a person more expert than you or to act in conjunction with you. Towards the end of the matter, a personality conflict between you and the client may suggest that the client might be better served using another lawyer. At trial, your duty to the court may require

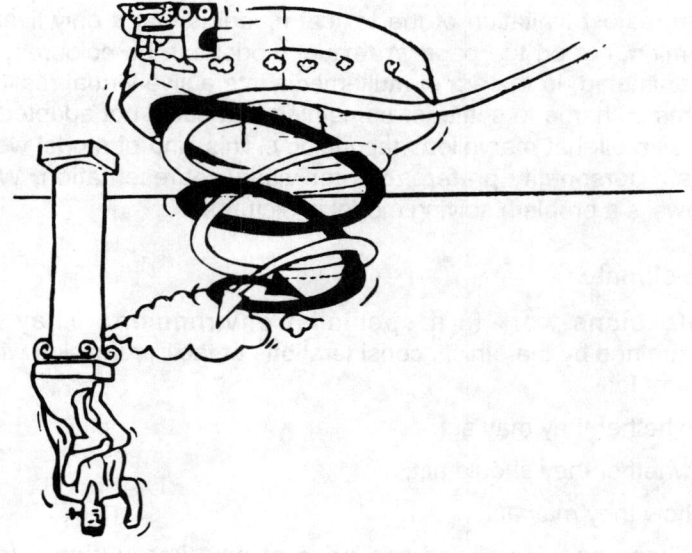

you to disclose information that your client does not want disclosed.

These factors are ever present, like the climate. The climate can change. It can also be ignored. Like the weather (see figure 9.2).

Figure 9.2

The content

The content of a legal problem comprises the client's objectives or proposals, the facts, law and whatever other information you might need to know (such as principles for plain language in drafting, or the history of the development of battery technology in a patent case). (The climate is also a kind of content but its special place warrants special treatment.) Since we are constantly turning over the content over in our minds, this seemed best represented as a wheel (see figure 9.3).

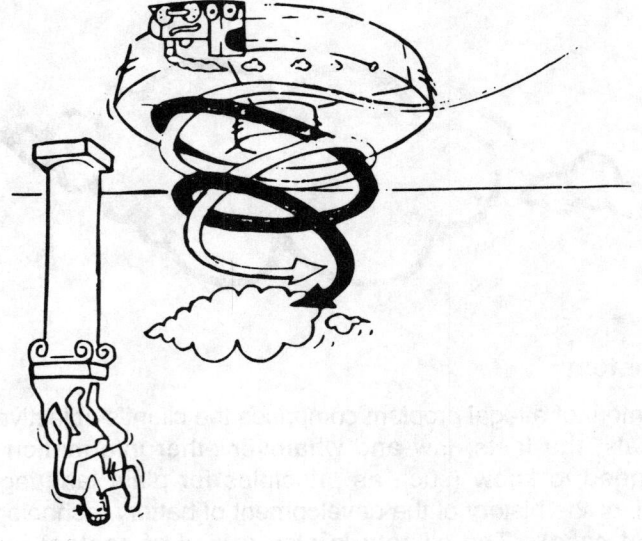

Figure 9.3

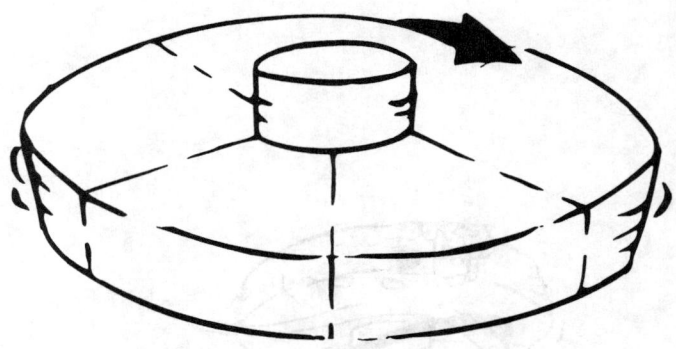

This wheel contains four segments to remind us of the four phases, each with the main questions to represent the focus of each phase:

- What
- Whether
- Why
- How

Change still remains at the heart of thought.

Action choices

So far the content has only been thought about, yet, as we have seen, legal problems require a conscious choice of what to do. Does the problem solver initiate contact by a phone call, a letter or a meeting? Does the legal thinker use an established procedure for dealing with the transaction or make up his or her own? Many actions might need to be taken to clarify content before the solution can be implemented, so the action needs to include talk. For action, I have selected a pre-computer icon – a

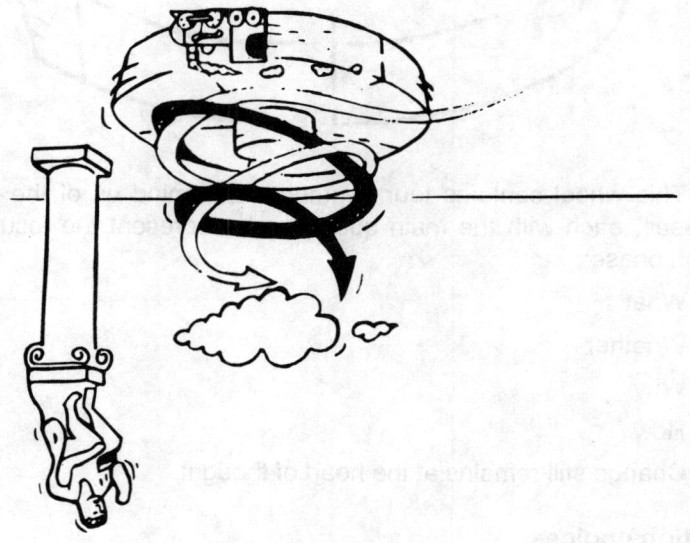

train. It is a steam train to remind us that talk is one of the choices
Under the train, we can include a checklist of the actions that we
can choose from, including the continuum of talk (see figure 9.4).

Figure 9.4

Steering and speed

The content wheel is turned and the actions are consciously
selected at each of the problem solving phases by thought. Rodin
has provided us with the icon for thought (see figure 9.5 overleaf).

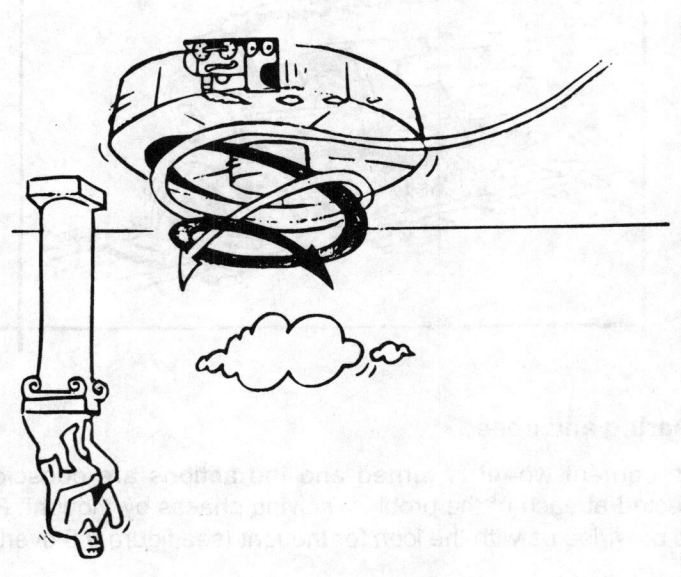

Figure 9.5

Chapters 5 to 8 list many tools for thought in expansionary and contractionary mode. Actually, in the text, I cheated a little. It is not easy to designate the thought tools as expansionary or contractionary. Often it depends on how they are used. Some of the thought tools include action such as brainstorming or mindmapping, while others are purely about what goes on in the mind, for example, deduction or analogy. In the absence of a proper taxonomy for all these thought tools, I have simply reproduced a summary checklist of all those dealt with in the book. The checklist begins with tools that only take place in the mind (and are peculiar to the thinker), and ending with those that are paired (such as the probability benefits matrix), or that are shared and therefore shade into action (such as flowcharts and checklists) (see figure 9.6).

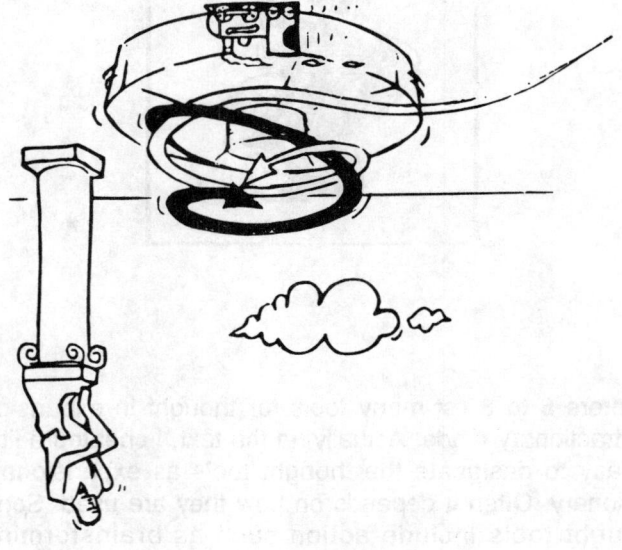

Figure 9.6

THOUGHT TOOLS

THOUGHT TOOLS
THOUGHT TOOLS

EXPANSIONARY
- BRAINSTORM
- ACTIVE LISTENING
- IMAGINING OTHER SIDE
- DOING A PROBLEM-SOLVING WALKAROUND
- NARRATIVE POSSIBILITIES
- CREATIVE POSSIBILITIES
  - BIGGER
  - SMALLER
  - MORE MONEY
  - LESS MONEY
  - DIFFERENT CLIENT
  - RANDOM WORD, PICTURE
- ASK OTHER LAWYERS
  - WHAT OTHER FIRMS DO
  - WHAT OTHER PROFESSIONS DO
- LOOK WIDER
- LOOK INTO FUTURE - ANTICIPATE
- MINDMAP

CONTRACTIONARY
- LAW AS AUTHORITY
- LAW AS LANGUAGE
- LAW AS LOGIC
- DEDUCTIVE SYLLOGISMS
- INDUCTIVE SYLLOGISMS
- RHETORICAL ARGUMENT
- FACTS - BELIEF
  - PERSUASIVE
  - EVIDENCE
- PROBABILITY BENEFITS MATRIX
- HYPOTHESIS IN QUESTION FORM
- COMPUTING THE ODDS - DECISION AREAS   ??
- CHRONOLOGY
- DIAGRAM
- FLOWCHART
- DECISION CHART
- PROJECT MANAGEMENT
  - PERT
  - GANT
  - CPM
- CHECKLIST

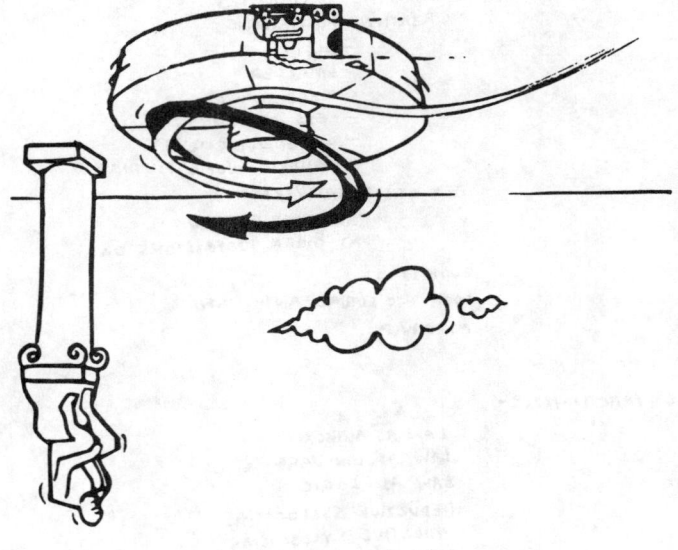

The moving model

Surrounded by the climate, the content wheel turns through thought and generates actions from the action list. Often a legal transaction starts off with broad content, refines and focuses the issues to its conclusion generating a gradually narrowing funnel shape (figure 9.7).

Figure 9.7

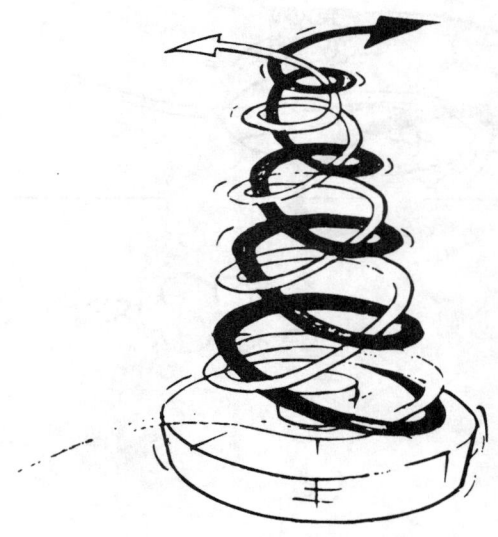

This would be the perfect litigation matter that takes the other side to your conclusion.

One can imagine other matters with other shapes. The easy matter that started off small might establish a mini-mountain range of several spirals going off in various directions. A commercial deal that starts off with both sides spiralling around each other in co-operation might spin off in opposite directions and never conclude.

For this model to move, your mind needs to animate it. Of course, this might not be your picture of a legal transaction at all. Perhaps this will stimulate you to draw your own.

The model as poster

Figure 9.8 is the depiction of the model as a poster is to remind you of all the things that you have read about in this book.

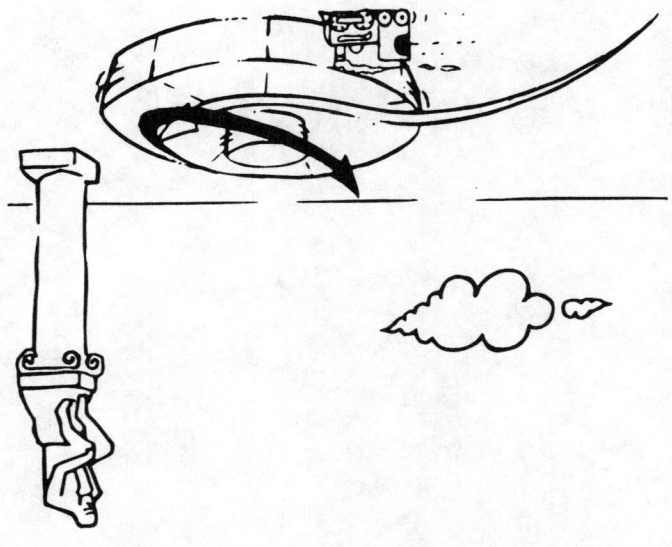

Figure 9.8

EVENTS (Action)

EVENTS (REaction)

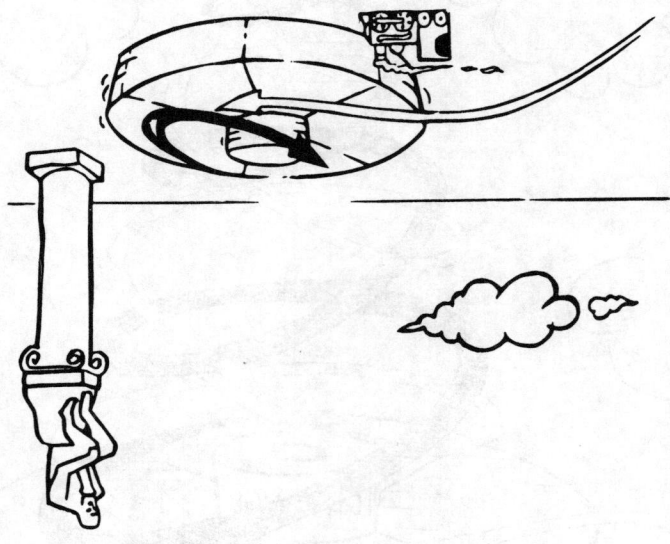

9.2.1   Turn the book upside down and back to front to animate the model

You do not need a television to enjoy the animations of Walt Disney. You can purchase small flip books that are animated by flicking the pages. Turn this book upside down and back to front. By flipping the first few pages you will have a moving model. It might even be the first piece of litigation that you have won! This is the Macintosh equivalent of the problem solving model to match the textual model above. This might appeal to more visual, conceptual personality types who want a reminder rather than a list and who enjoy whimsy.

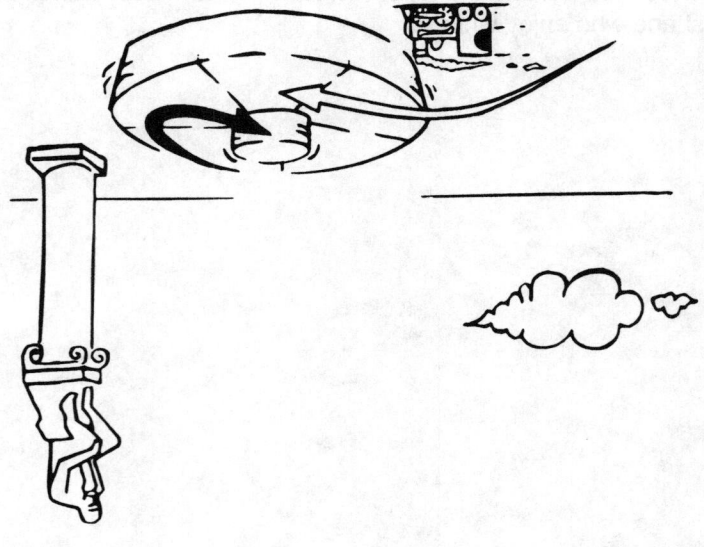

CHAPTER

10 Exercises

This book is presented in such a way that you have to work through it, not just read it. As you read it, you will naturally call to mind things that you have read in the paper, seen on television and tried to do while studying law.

For those who would like to do some follow-up work, here are some suggestions.

Chapter 1: From method to mêlée

Read Charles Sampford's *Disorder of Law*, taking particular note of the many charts and line images.

Chapter 2: The lawyer inside the problem I

Try out some of the visual material on your friends and family. You will be truly amazed at the inconsistency of results.

Lay your head face down on a piece of paper and trace the outline. Then have a hot shower to fog up the mirror in the bathroom. Trace around the outline of your face in the mirror. Is the outline in the mirror bigger or smaller than the actual size? What accounts for the difference?

Visit the local magistrates' court to see judgment under uncertainty in action. Attend the closing submissions to a jury of an advocate that you admire. See the preference for anecdote above probability in action.

Chapter 3: The lawyer inside the problem II

Select a judgment from a judge you admire. Read as much as you can about that judge. Compare that judgment with a judgment that you disapprove of from another judge. Read as much as you can about that judge. Think about the sort of personality factors

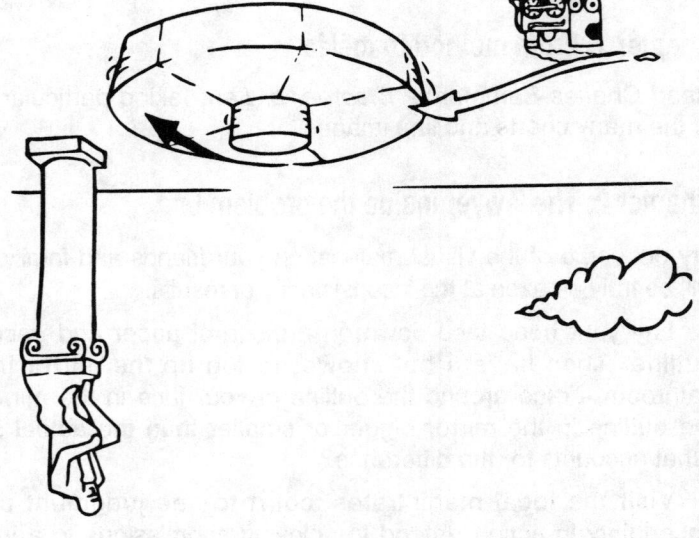

that colour the way they express their judgments as well as the content of the decision.

Complete a personality index for yourself. They are often made in the context of selecting preferred employment and, for recent graduates, might be helpful in that context.

Borrow Kurosawa's film *Rashamon* from the local video library. It shows four versions of one story from the perspectives of the different protagonists.

Chapter 4: Back to a model for legal problem solving

Try out some of the problem solving models when next solving a legal problem to determine the usefulness of a step by step heuristic to give you ideas. Run a meeting using one of the legal models in which every participant consciously works through the process at the same stage and at the same pace.

Chapter 5: Situation analysis

Prepare a mind map of one of the law subjects that you liked during your legal studies. Include drawings and colour.

Write down your analysis of the facts and law in the next few issues that you look at in the form of a conscious hypothesis in no more than 35 words. Prepare a list of questions setting out factors to be confirmed, investigated or researched.

Chair a meeting in which a number of lawyers attempt to solve a problem. Try out the expansionary mode by brainstorming and using random images and words. Discipline the meeting so that they will really try these techniques, rather than using the meeting to evaluate what they refuse to try (good luck!).

Chapter 6: Problem analysis

Take an account of facts in a case. Write a script that could be filmed using a camcorder. Ask your friends to act out the script

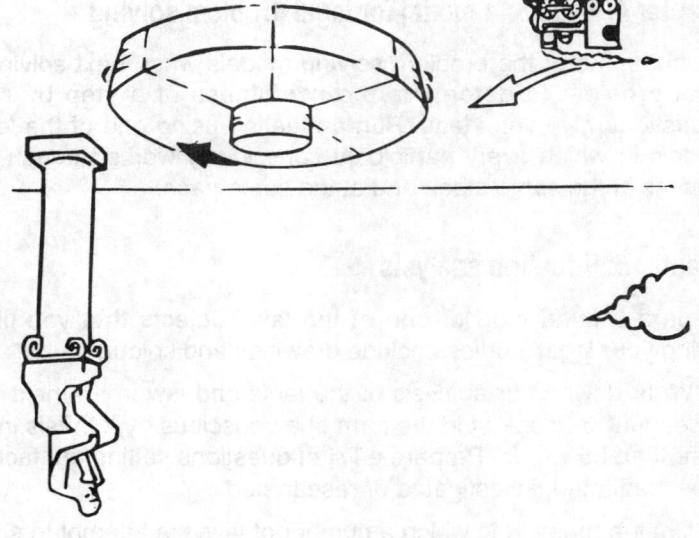

and film it. Play it back. Which portions were given emphasis by the law? Which portions were omitted? What did you have to do to turn the recount of facts into the narration of a story? How did the story affect the people around you?

Take a legal judgment and rewrite the logic of the decision in the form of a series of syllogisms or a series of inductive statements.

Find a case that presents a disagreement about language as an argument about logic.

Chapter 7: Solution analysis

Use an area of law in which you are particularly interested and in which other professionals find involvement. Family law, building disputes, mergers and acquisitions and tax questions, are some possible examples. Interview the other professionals about how they would define or describe the problems for the clients in those cases. What solutions do the other professionals see that would deal with all the clients problems? If the other professionals were to design a means of delivering interdisciplinary advice – a kind of one stop shop – how would they design it?

Identify a statute that sets out the criteria to be taken into account in making a decision. Set out the procedure in the form of step by step questions, preferably having only a yes/no choice for your answer.

Chapter 8: Implementation analysis

Interview a systems analyst. Find out how they use flowcharts to analyse an information system.

Interview a management consultant from a world-wide consultancy such as Anderson Consulting or McKinsey's. They do not write letters of advice to clients although they frequently act in a problem solving role. What techniques do they use to advise the client and to map out a process of implementing a plan?

Interview an auditor involved in a large audit. How do they structure the job so that many people can work on it together without overlap and confusion?

Design a new checklist for taking instructions in your firm or organisation.

Identify a statute that sets out a procedure to be followed. Rewrite the procedure in plain language, setting out the steps to be taken in the order in which they have to be taken and by whom. Experiment with setting out the procedure using a table specifying the person to take the action, the action to be taken, time specifications and standards to be complied with. Then represent the procedure as a flowchart or a time line.